THE PHO COOKBOOK

Colin Robinett

Genuine **250+** Recipe and Crucial Methods for Mastering the Famous Noodle Soup of Vietnam

COPYRIGHT 2024 - ALL RIGHTS RESERVED

COOKBOOK

The reproduction, duplication, or transfer of the content in this book is strictly prohibited without the explicit written consent of the author or publisher. The publisher and author disclaim any liability or legal responsibility for damages, reparation, or financial loss, whether direct or indirect, arising from the material contained in this book.

DISCLAIMER NOTICE

This booklet is intended solely for educational and entertainment purposes. While every effort has been made to provide accurate, up-to-date, reliable, and complete information, no guarantees, whether expressed or implied, are made. The author does not provide legal, financial, medical, or professional advice, and readers are strongly advised to seek the advice of licensed experts before implementing any strategies outlined in this book. By reading this document, the reader agrees that the author is not liable for any direct or indirect damages resulting from the use of the information, including errors, omissions, or inaccuracies.

LEGAL NOTICE

This book is protected by copyright and is designated for personal use only. Any modification, distribution, sale, quoting, or paraphrasing of any part of this book without the explicit permission of the author or publisher is strictly prohibited

ALL IMAGES ARE SOURCED FROM WWW.SHUTTERSTOCK.COM

INDEX

INTRODUCTION TO PHO 9	
TOOLS AND EQUIPMENT 10	
CHAPTER: 1 PHO BROTH BASICS: 11	

- Classic Beef Pho Broth 11
- Fragrant Chicken Pho Broth 11
- Mushroom Broth (Vegetarian) 11
- Rich Seafood Broth 12
- Spicy Lemongrass Broth 12
- Vegan Pho Broth with Tofu 13
- Pork Bone Broth 13
- Ginger-infused broth 13
- Five-Spice Vegetable Broth 13
- Turmeric Coconut Broth 14
- Pho Broth with Star Anise 14
- Clear Vegetable Broth 14
- Vietnamese Beef Bone Broth 15
- Citrusy Chicken Pho Broth 15
- Herbal Vegetable Broth 15
- Beef Bone Marrow Broth 16
- Smoky Mushroom Broth 16
- Fish Sauce Infused Broth 16
- Red Curry Coconut Broth 17
- Pho Broth with Cinnamon Sticks 17
- Chicken Feet Broth 17
- Garlic and Onion Broth 18
- Szechuan Peppercorn Broth 18
- Beef Knuckle Broth 18
- Lemongrass Coconut Broth 19
- Spicy Beef Pho Broth 19
- Miso Ginger Broth 19
- Roasted Vegetable Broth 19
- Beef Shank Broth 20
- Shallot and Bay Leaf Broth 20
- Tomato-based Broth 21
- Thai Basil Infused Broth 21
- Fennel Seed Broth 21
- Roasted Chicken Bone Broth 22
- Lemongrass Tofu Broth 22
- Peppercorn Chicken Broth 22
- Seaweed and Mushroom Broth 23
- Cilantro Lime Broth 23
- Shiitake Ginger Broth 23
- Coconut Curry Broth 24

CHAPTER: 2 BEEF PHO VARIATIONS: 24

- Traditional Beef Pho (Pho Bo) 24
- Beef Meatball Pho (Pho Bo Vien) 24
- Beef Tendon Pho (Pho Gan) 25
- Beef Tripe Pho (Pho Sach) 25
- Beef Flank Pho (Pho Nam) 25
- Beef Shank Pho (Pho Gau) 26
- Spicy Beef Pho 26
- Lemongrass Beef Pho 26
- Black Pepper Beef Pho 27
- Five-Spice Beef Pho 27
- Garlic Beef Pho 28
- Satay Beef Pho 28
- Ginger Beef Pho 28
- Coconut Beef Pho 29
- Hoisin Beef Pho 29
- Sriracha Beef Pho 30
- Basil Beef Pho 30
- Curry Beef Pho 30
- Kimchi Beef Pho 31
- Red Wine Beef Pho 31
- Pineapple Beef Pho 31
- Honey Soy Beef Pho 32
- Teriyaki Beef Pho 32
- Citrus Beef Pho 33
- Wasabi Beef Pho 33
- Pesto Beef Pho 33
- Cilantro Lime Beef Pho 34
- Chipotle Beef Pho 34
- Balsamic Glazed Beef Pho 35
- Mustard Seed Beef Pho 35
- Szechuan Beef Pho 35
- Mango Beef Pho 36
- Paprika Beef Pho 36
- Jalapeno Beef Pho 36
- Truffle Beef Pho 37
- Sesame Beef Pho 37
- Cumin Beef Pho 38
- Rosemary Beef Pho 38

CHAPTER: 3 CHICKEN PHO VARIATIONS: 38

- Classic Chicken Pho 38
- Spicy Lemongrass Chicken Pho 39
- Coconut Curry Chicken Pho 39
- Ginger Chicken Pho with Bok Choy 40
- Five-Spice Chicken Pho 40
- Sriracha Chicken Pho 40
- Cilantro-Lime Chicken Pho 41
- Thai Basil Chicken Pho 41
- Roasted Garlic Chicken Pho 41
- Smoked Paprika Chicken Pho 42
- Honey Sesame Chicken Pho 42
- Teriyaki Chicken Pho 43
- Chipotle Chicken Pho 43
- Szechuan Pepper Chicken Pho 43
- Satay Chicken Pho 44

Mango Chicken Pho	44
Pineapple Chicken Pho	45
Cashew Chicken Pho	45
Peanut Chicken Pho	46
Lemongrass-Coconut Chicken Pho	46
Green Curry Chicken Pho	46
Red Curry Chicken Pho	47
Tom Yum Chicken Pho	47
Lemongrass-Ginger Chicken Pho	48
Lemongrass-Chili Chicken Pho	48
Lemongrass-Coconut Curry Chicken Pho	48
Lemongrass-Cilantro Chicken Pho	49
Lemongrass-Mint Chicken Pho	49
Lemongrass-Galangal Chicken Pho	49
Lemongrass-Thai Chili Chicken Pho	50
Lemongrass-Soy Chicken Pho	50
Lemongrass-Galangal Chicken Pho	51
Lemongrass-Sesame Chicken Pho	51
Lemongrass-Tamarind Chicken Pho	51
Lemongrass-Vinegar Chicken Pho	52
Lemongrass-Cornstarch Chicken Pho	52

CHAPTER: 4 VEGETARIAN AND VEGAN PHO: 53

Tofu Pho	53
Mushroom Pho	53
Vegetable Pho	54
Jackfruit Pho	54
Seitan Pho	54
Eggplant Pho	55
Tempeh Pho	55
Lentil Pho	56
Spinach Pho	56
Kale Pho	56
Broccoli Pho	57
Cauliflower Pho	57
Bell Pepper Pho	58
Snap Pea Pho	58
Carrot Pho	58
Zucchini Pho	59
Sweet Potato Pho	59
Pumpkin Pho	60
Butternut Squash Pho	60
Coconut Curry Tofu Pho	60
Thai Basil Tofu Pho	61
Lemongrass-Ginger Tofu Pho	61
Lemongrass-Chili Tofu Pho	62
Lemongrass-Coconut Tofu Pho	62
Lemongrass-Cilantro Tofu Pho	62
Lemongrass-Kaffir Lime Tofu Pho	63
Lemongrass-Galangal Tofu Pho	63
Lemongrass-Thai Chili Tofu Pho	64
Lemongrass-Soy Tofu Pho	64
Lemongrass-Fish Sauce Tofu Pho	64
Lemongrass-Oyster Sauce Tofu Pho	65
Lemongrass-Hoisin Tofu Pho	65

Lemongrass-Sesame Tofu Pho	66
Lemongrass-Tamarind Tofu Pho	66
Lemongrass-Vinegar Tofu Pho	66
Lemongrass-Cornstarch Tofu Pho	67
Lemongrass-Black Bean Tofu Pho	67
Lemongrass-Garlic Tofu Pho	67

CHAPTER: 5 SEAFOOD PHO CREATIONS: 68

Shrimp Pho	68
Crab Pho	68
Fish Pho	69
Clam Pho	69
Scallop Pho	70
Lobster Pho	70
Squid Pho	70
Octopus Pho	71
Mussel Pho	71
Mixed Seafood Pho	72
Coconut Curry Shrimp Pho	72
Thai Basil Shrimp Pho	72
Lemongrass-Ginger Shrimp Pho	73
Lemongrass-Chili Shrimp Pho	73
Lemongrass-Coconut Shrimp Pho	74
Lemongrass-Cilantro Shrimp Pho	74
Lemongrass-Mint Shrimp Pho	74
Lemongrass-Basil Shrimp Pho	75
Lemongrass-Kaffir Lime Shrimp Pho	75
Lemongrass-Galangal Shrimp Pho	75
Lemongrass-Thai Chili Shrimp Pho	76
Lemongrass-Soy Shrimp Pho	76
Lemongrass-Fish Sauce Shrimp Pho	76
Lemongrass-Oyster Sauce Shrimp Pho	77
Lemongrass-Hoisin Shrimp Pho	77
Lemongrass-Sesame Shrimp Pho	78
Lemongrass-Tamarind Shrimp Pho	78
Lemongrass-Vinegar Shrimp Pho	78
Lemongrass-Cornstarch Shrimp Pho	79
Lemongrass-Black Bean Shrimp Pho	79
Lemongrass-Garlic Shrimp Pho	79
Lemongrass-Onion Shrimp Pho	80
Lemongrass-Carrot Shrimp Pho	80
Lemongrass-Broccoli Shrimp Pho	80
Lemongrass-Cauliflower Shrimp Pho	81
Lemongrass-Bell Pepper Shrimp Pho	81
Lemongrass-Snap Pea Shrimp Pho	81
Lemongrass-Zucchini Shrimp Pho	82
Lemongrass-Sweet Potato Shrimp Pho	82
Lemongrass-Pumpkin Shrimp Pho	82

CHAPTER: 6 REGIONAL PHO STYLES: 83

Northern Style Beef Pho (Phở Bắc)	83
Southern Style Beef Pho (Phở Nam)	83
Central Style Beef Pho (Phở Trung)	83
Hanoi Style Beef Pho (Phở Hà Nội)	84
Hoi An Style Beef Pho (Phở Hội An)	84

- Nha Trang Style Beef Pho (Phở Nha Trang) 85
- Vung Tau Style Beef Pho (Phở Vũng Tàu) 85
- Phan Thiet Style Beef Pho (Phở Phan Thiết) 85
- Mekong Delta Style Beef Pho (Phở Đồng Bằng Sông Cửu Long) 86
- Central Highlands Style Beef Pho (Phở Tây Nguyên) 86
- Quy Nhon Style Beef Pho (Phở Quy Nhơn) 86
- Bac Lieu Style Beef Pho (Phở Bạc Liêu) 87
- Vinh Long Style Beef Pho (Phở Vĩnh Long) 87
- Ha Long Style Beef Pho (Phở Hạ Long) 87
- Hai Phong Style Beef Pho (Phở Hải Phòng) 88
- Dong Thap Style Beef Pho (Phở Đồng Tháp) 88
- Soc Trang Style Beef Pho (Phở Sóc Trăng) 89
- Tra Vinh Style Beef Pho (Phở Trà Vinh) 89
- Bac Ninh Style Beef Pho (Phở Bắc Ninh) 89
- Bac Giang Style Beef Pho (Phở Bắc Giang) 90
- Lemongrass-Kaffir Lime Shrimp Pho 90
- Lemongrass-Galangal Shrimp Pho 91
- Lai Chau Style Beef Pho 91
- Dien Bien Style Beef Pho 91
- Lang Son Style Beef Pho 92
- Thai Nguyen Style Beef Pho 92
- Ha Nam Style Beef Pho 93
- Nam Dinh Style Beef Pho 93
- Thanh Hoa Style Beef Pho 93
- Nghe An Style Beef Pho 94
- Ha Tinh Style Beef Pho 94
- Quang Binh Style Beef Pho 95
- Quang Tri-Style Beef Pho 95
- Thua Thien Hue Style Beef Pho 96
- Quang Nam Style Beef Pho 96
- Quang Ngai Style Beef Pho 96

CHAPTER: 7 PHO GARNISHES AND CONDIMENTS: 97

- Quick-Pickled Fresh Bean Sprouts 97
- Classic Beef Pho with Lime Wedges 97
- Chicken Pho with Sliced Jalapeños 98
- Vegetarian Pho with Thinly Sliced Scallions 98
- Quick-Pickled Bean Sprouts 98
- Classic Lime Beef Pho 98
- Spicy Jalapeño Chicken Pho 99
- Scallion Ginger Beef Pho 99
- Fried Shallots 100
- Thai Chili Peppers (Chili Oil) 100
- Hoisin Sauce 100
- Homemade Sriracha Sauce 101
- Homemade Fish Sauce 101
- Homemade Soy Sauce 101
- Oyster Sauce 102
- Chili Garlic Sauce 102
- Pickled Garlic 102
- Pickled Jalapeños 102
- Pickled Carrots 103
- Pickled Daikon Radish 103
- Sliced Red Chilies 103
- Crushed Peanuts 104
- Fried Garlic 104
- Chili Oil 104
- Sesame Oil 104
- Rice Vinegar 105
- Homemade Mirin 105
- Brown Sugar Beef Pho 105
- Pho with Red Wine Vinegar Reduction 106
- Worcestershire Sauce Chicken Pho 106
- Sambal Oelek 106
- Gochujang 107
- Kimchi 107
- Furikake 107

INTRODUCTION TO PHO

In the heart of Vietnamese cuisine lies the soul-warming dish known as Pho, a culinary masterpiece that combines fragrant broth, tender meats, and fresh herbs in a symphony of flavors that has captivated food lovers around the globe. "The Pho Cookbook" serves as a comprehensive guide to this beloved dish, offering readers an immersive journey into its rich history, cultural significance, and the artistry behind its preparation. From the bustling streets of Hanoi to the vibrant markets of Saigon, Pho is more than just a meal; it is a reflection of Vietnam's complex history and the resilience of its people. To make sure that everyone can enjoy making and eating this famous meal, this handbook offers a wide range of recipes, from classic beef pho to creative vegetarian alternatives. With detailed instructions, expert tips, and insights into the nuances of authentic Pho preparation, readers will learn how to simmer the perfect broth, select the right noodles, and balance the delicate flavors that define this dish. The book also delves into the ritual of Pho eating, highlighting the communal aspect of sharing a bowl with family and friends, making it a celebration of culture and companionship. Whether you are a seasoned Pho enthusiast or a curious newcomer, "The Pho Cookbook" invites you to explore the depths of Vietnamese culinary tradition and discover the magic of Pho in your own kitchen.

TOOLS AND EQUIPMENT

In "The Pho Cookbook," the section on Tools and Equipment is meticulously designed to ensure readers are well-equipped to embark on their Pho-making journey. Understanding that the essence of crafting an authentic Pho lies in both the technique and the tools used, the book provides a detailed overview of the essential kitchenware needed to replicate the traditional flavors of this Vietnamese staple. Central to the Pho preparation process is a large stockpot, which is crucial for simmering the broth to achieve its characteristic depth and clarity. A fine mesh strainer or cheesecloth is recommended for skimming impurities, ensuring the broth remains clear and flavorful.

To serve Pho in the authentic manner, the cookbook suggests having a set of deep bowls that retain heat well, along with soup spoons and chopsticks for the complete dining experience. A sharp chef's knife is vital for thinly slicing meats, while a mandoline or a sharp knife is suggested for cutting vegetables and herbs with precision. The book also highlights the importance of having a small spice bag or tea infuser for the pho spices, allowing their flavors to infuse the broth without leaving residues.

For those looking to explore beyond the basics, "The Pho Cookbook" introduces specialized equipment like noodle baskets for those who prefer to pre-cook their noodles separately and a ladle for evenly distributing the hot broth over the prepared bowls. Emphasizing accessibility, the book offers practical advice on finding suitable alternatives for specialized tools, ensuring that the joy of pho-making is within reach for everyone, regardless of their kitchen setup. With this comprehensive guide to the necessary tools and equipment, readers are well-prepared to delve into the art of Pho, bringing the authentic taste of Vietnam into their homes.

CHAPTER: 1 PHO BROTH BASICS:

CLASSIC BEEF PHO BROTH

Preparation Time: 30 minutes || Cooking Time: 6 hours || Servings: 6

Ingredients:

5 lbs beef bones (a mix of marrow and knuckle bones)	1 large onion, halved and unpeeled
1 4-inch piece of ginger, halved lengthwise	3-4 cinnamon sticks
3-star anise	3 cloves
1 cardamom pod	1 tablespoon coriander seeds
1 tablespoon salt	1 tablespoon sugar
1/4 cup fish sauce	6 quarts water
Fresh rice noodles for serving	Thinly sliced beef (sirloin, brisket, or eye round) for serving
Optional garnishes: lime wedges, fresh herbs (cilantro, basil, mint), bean sprouts, sliced chili peppers, hoisin sauce, and sriracha	

Instructions:

(1) Charring onion and ginger start. Grill or broil them till slightly charred. Allow 5 minutes. Wash off darkened skin. **(2)** Cover beef bones in a large stockpot with water. Boil for 10 minutes. Rinse bones with warm water. Clean and return bones to pot. **(3)** Put the cleaned bones, charred onion, ginger, cinnamon sticks, star anise, cloves, cardamom pod, coriander seeds, salt, sugar, and fish sauce in a saucepan with 6 quarts of water. Boil then simmers. Skim any foam or fat after 6 hours of simmering. **(4)** Pass the broth through a fine-mesh strainer into a clean pot. Waste solids. **(5)** Follow package instructions to cook rice noodles. Layer noodles in bowls, top with thinly sliced meat (the hot broth will cook it), then pour hot soup over. Optional garnishes.

FRAGRANT CHICKEN PHO BROTH

Preparation Time: 20 minutes || Cooking Time: 1.5 hours || Servings: 6

Ingredients:

1 whole chicken (about 4-5 lbs)	1 large onion, halved and unpeeled
1 4-inch piece of ginger, halved lengthwise	3-4 cinnamon sticks
3-star anise	3 cloves
1 cardamom pod	1 tablespoon coriander seeds
1 tablespoon salt	1 tablespoon sugar
1/4 cup fish sauce	6 quarts water
Fresh rice noodles for serving	Optional garnishes: lime wedges, fresh herbs (cilantro, basil, mint), bean sprouts, sliced chili peppers, hoisin sauce, and sriracha

Instructions:

(1) Char the onion and ginger like in Classic Beef Pho. **(2)** Cover the entire chicken with water in a large stockpot. Cook for 10 minutes at a boil. Remove chicken, drain water, and rinse pot. **(3)** Put the chicken, 6 quarts of new water, the charred onion, ginger, and the other spices, salt, sugar, and fish sauce back in the saucepan. Heat to boiling, then simmer. Cook chicken until done, about 1.5 hours. **(4)** Remove chicken from soup and cool. Like the beef recipe, strain the broth. **(5)** Serve shredded chicken with rice noodles and hot broth. Garnish as desired.

MUSHROOM BROTH (VEGETARIAN)

Preparation Time: 20 minutes || Cooking Time: 1.5 hours || Servings: 6

Ingredients:

2 lbs mixed mushrooms (such as shiitake, portobello, and cremini), roughly	1 large onion, halved and unpeeled

chopped
1 4-inch piece of ginger, halved lengthwise
3-star anise
1 cardamom pod
1 tablespoon salt
1/4 cup soy sauce
Fresh rice noodles for serving

3-4 cinnamon sticks
3 cloves
1 tablespoon coriander seeds
1 tablespoon sugar
6 quarts water
Optional garnishes: lime wedges, fresh herbs (cilantro, basil, mint), bean sprouts, sliced chili peppers, hoisin sauce, and sriracha

Instructions:

(1) As stated in the earlier recipes, char the ginger and onion. **(2)** Add the mushrooms, ginger, and charred onion to a large stockpot along with the remaining spices, sugar, salt, and soy sauce. When the water reaches a boil, add six quarts. **(3)** Simmer the mixture for one and a half hours without a lid, making sure to scrape any froth that peaks at the top. **(4)** Using a fine-mesh filter, strain the broth into a fresh saucepan. Get rid of solids. **(5)** Together with your preferred toppings, serve the soup over cooked rice noodles.

RICH SEAFOOD BROTH

Preparation Time: 20 minutes || Cooking Time: 1 hour 30 minutes || Servings: 4-6

Ingredients:

2 pounds mixed seafood (shrimp, squid, mussels, and fish bones)
4 cloves garlic, smashed
3 liters water

1 tablespoon salt
1 inch ginger, sliced
1 cinnamon stick

1 large onion, quartered

2 carrots, chopped

2 tablespoons fish sauce
2 teaspoons sugar
3-star anise

Instructions:

(1) Under cold running water, rinse the seafood and fish bones. **(2)** Water, seafood, fish bones, onion, garlic, carrots, ginger, star anise, and cinnamon sticks should all be combined in a big saucepan. **(3)** Heat to a boil over high heat, then turn down the heat. Skim any froth that rises to the surface and simmer for one hour. **(4)** Pour the broth into a fresh saucepan by straining it through a fine-mesh strainer. To extract as much liquid as possible, press down on the solids. **(5)** Add sugar, salt, and fish sauce to season the soup. Taste and adjust the seasoning. **(6)** Serve hot as the foundation for your pho recipes with seafood.

SPICY LEMONGRASS BROTH

Preparation Time: 15 minutes || Cooking Time: 1 hour || Servings: 4-6

Ingredients:

1-gallon water

4 cloves garlic, smashed
2 tablespoons fish sauce
2 teaspoons sugar
1 inch ginger, sliced

2 stalks of lemongrass, tough outer layers removed and smashed
1 large onion, quartered
1 tablespoon salt

2 bird's eye chilies, sliced (adjust to taste)
3 kaffir lime leaves

Instructions:

(1) Put water, kaffir lime leaves, onion, ginger, garlic, and lemongrass in a big saucepan. Bring over high heat to a boil. **(2)** For forty-five minutes, simmer over low heat. **(3)** Add the fish sauce, sugar, salt, and bird's eye chilies. Simmer for fifteen minutes more. **(4)** Pour the broth into a fresh saucepan by straining it through a fine-mesh strainer. Throw away the solids. **(5)** Taste and adjust the seasoning. The flavors of the broth should be harmoniously hot, salty, and sweet. **(6)** Serve hot as the foundation for your hot meals of spicy lemongrass pho.

VEGAN PHO BROTH WITH TOFU

Preparation Time: 20 minutes || Cooking Time: 1 hour || Servings: 4-6

Ingredients:

1-gallon vegetable stock	2 large onions, quartered
4 cloves garlic, smashed	1 inch ginger, sliced
2 carrots, chopped	1 tablespoon soy sauce
1 tablespoon salt	2 teaspoons sugar
2-star anise	1 cinnamon stick
1 block of firm tofu, cut up into cubes	Fresh herbs (cilantro, basil) for garnish

Instructions:

(1) Vegetable stock, carrots, star anise, garlic, onions, and cinnamon stick should all be combined in a big saucepan. Bring over high heat to a boil. **(2)** For forty-five minutes, simmer over low heat. **(3)** Pour the broth into a fresh saucepan by straining it through a fine-mesh strainer. Throw away the solids. **(4)** Add sugar, salt, and soy sauce to season the soup. Taste and adjust the seasoning. **(5)** Tofu cubes should be added to the broth and cooked for a further fifteen minutes so that the tofu may absorb the flavors. **(6)** Garnish with fresh herbs and serve hot.

PORK BONE BROTH

Preparation Time: 30 minutes || Cooking Time: 6 hours || Servings: 8

Ingredients:

3 lbs pork bones	1 onion, halved and charred
4 cloves garlic, smashed	2-inch piece of ginger, sliced and charred
2-star anise	1 cinnamon stick
6 cloves	Salt, to taste
12 cups water	

Instructions:

(1) Clock in 425°F (220°C) in the oven. Roast the pig bones for 20 minutes, or until browned, on a baking sheet. **(2)** The roasted bones, water, star anise, cinnamon stick, cloves, charred onion, garlic, and ginger should all be added to a large stockpot. **(3)** Turn down the heat to a simmer after it boils. Skimming off any foam or other contaminants that come to the surface gets rid of them. **(4)** For six hours, simmer the mixture uncovered, adding extra water as needed to keep the bones immersed. **(5)** Put the broth in a clean saucepan after straining it through a fine-mesh strainer. Add salt to taste to season. **(6)** After letting it cool, refrigerate. To reheat and serve, remove the hardened fat off the top.

GINGER-INFUSED BROTH

Preparation Time: 15 minutes || Cooking Time: 1 hour || Servings: 6

Ingredients:

8 cups chicken or vegetable stock	4-inch piece of ginger, thinly sliced
2 cloves garlic, minced	1 lemongrass stalk, bruised
2 green onions, chopped	Salt and pepper, to taste

Instructions:

(1) Put the stock, ginger, garlic, and lemongrass in a big saucepan. **(2)** If you want the ginger to flavor the soup, bring it to a boil and then turn down the heat to a simmer for 45 minutes. **(3)** Simmer for a further fifteen minutes after adding the green onions. **(4)** To taste, add salt and pepper for seasoning. **(5)** Pour the broth either straight into serving cups or into a clean saucepan after straining through a fine mesh screen.

FIVE-SPICE VEGETABLE BROTH

Preparation Time: 20 minutes || Cooking Time: 45 minutes || Servings: 6

Ingredients:

8 cups vegetable stock	1 onion, chopped
2 carrots, chopped	2 celery stalks, chopped

1 tsp Chinese five-spice powder	1 bay leaf
Salt and pepper, to taste	

Instructions:

(1) Add the onion, carrots, celery, five-spice powder, bay leaf, and vegetable stock to a large saucepan. **(2)** When it starts to boil, turn down the heat and let it cook for 45 minutes. **(3)** To taste, add salt and pepper for seasoning. **(4)** Pour the broth either straight into serving cups or into a clean saucepan after straining through a fine mesh screen. Throw away the solids.

TURMERIC COCONUT BROTH

Preparation Time: 15 minutes || Cooking Time: 30 minutes || Servings: 4

Ingredients:

4 cups vegetable stock	1 can (14 oz) coconut milk
1-inch piece of ginger, grated	1 tsp turmeric powder
1 clove garlic, minced	1 lime, juiced
Salt and pepper, to taste	Fresh cilantro for garnish

Instructions:

(1) Ginger, turmeric, garlic, coconut milk, and vegetable stock should all be combined in a big saucepan. **(2)** Start by boiling it. Then lower the heat and let it cook for 20 minutes. **(3)** After adding the lime juice, season to taste with salt and pepper. **(4)** Simmer for a further ten minutes. **(5)** Garnish with fresh cilantro and serve hot.

PHO BROTH WITH STAR ANISE

Preparation Time: 15 minutes || Cooking Time: 6 hours || Servings: 6

Ingredients:

2 onions, halved and charred	4-inch piece of ginger, halved and charred
3 cinnamon sticks	5-star anise
3 cloves	1 cardamom pod
1 tablespoon coriander seeds	6 quarts water
1 1/2 pounds of chicken bones or beef bones	1 tablespoon salt
2 tablespoons fish sauce	1 tablespoon sugar

Instructions:

(1) Clock in 425°F (220°C) in the oven. Roast onions and ginger on a baking sheet for 15 minutes until browned. **(2)** Toast coriander seeds, cinnamon, star anise, cloves, and cardamom for 3–4 minutes in a dry pan over medium heat until fragrant. **(3)** Put water, ginger, charred onions, toasted spices, and bones in a big pot. Boil on high, then simmer. **(4)** If any dirt comes to the surface, skim it off. Stir in the sugar, salt, and fish sauce. Simmer for around six hours without cover. **(5)** Remove the particles from the broth by straining it through a fine-mesh strainer. Modify the seasoning as needed.

CLEAR VEGETABLE BROTH

Preparation Time: 10 minutes || Cooking Time: 1 hour || Servings: 4

Ingredients:

8 cups water	2 carrots, chopped
2 stalks celery, chopped	1 onion, quartered
2 tomatoes, quartered	1 teaspoon black peppercorns
1 bay leaf	2 cloves garlic, crushed
Salt to taste	

Instructions:

(1) Put all ingredients into a big saucepan and stir. Over high heat, bring to a boil and then lower the heat to a simmer. **(2)** Simmer for around one hour, or until the flavors have combined and the broth has decreased by about 25%. **(3)** Remove the particles from the broth by straining it through a fine-mesh strainer. Use salt to adjust the seasoning as necessary.

VIETNAMESE BEEF BONE BROTH

Preparation Time: 15 minutes || Cooking Time: 8 to 10 hours || Servings: 6

Ingredients:

- 4 pounds of beef bones (a mix of marrow and knuckle bones)
- 2 onions, halved and charred
- 4-inch piece of ginger, halved and charred
- 5-star anise
- 3 cinnamon sticks
- 4 cloves
- 1 tablespoon coriander seeds
- 6 quarts water
- 1 tablespoon salt
- 2 tablespoons fish sauce
- 1 tablespoon sugar
- 1 piece of rock sugar (about 2 ounces)

Instructions:

(1) Clock in 425°F (220°C) in the oven. For consistent browning, roast beef bones on a baking sheet for an hour, flipping once. **(2)** For the final fifteen minutes of roasting, sear the onions and ginger in the oven next to the bones. **(3)** The roasted bones, charred onions, ginger, star anise, cinnamon, cloves, and coriander seeds should all be added to a big saucepan. Bring the water to a boil while covering. **(4)** Skim any scum that comes to the surface and reduce to a simmer. Stir in the sugar, rock sugar, salt, and fish sauce. **(5)** Simmer for eight to ten hours over low heat, skimming the top now and again. **(6)** Remove the particles from the broth by straining it through a fine-mesh strainer. If needed, adjust the seasoning.

CITRUSY CHICKEN PHO BROTH

Preparation Time: 20 minutes || Cooking Time: 1 hour || Servings: 4

Ingredients:

- 1 large onion, peeled and halved
- 1 4-inch piece of ginger, halved lengthwise
- 2 lbs chicken bones or wings
- 10 cups water
- 2 tablespoons fish sauce
- 1 tablespoon sugar
- 1 small bunch cilantro
- 3-star anise
- 2 cinnamon sticks
- 4 cloves
- Zest of 1 lime
- Zest of 1 orange
- Salt, to taste

Instructions:

(1) Slightly blacken the onion and ginger by grilling them over an open flame or under the broiler for around five minutes. **(2)** Add the charred onion and ginger to a large saucepan with the fish sauce, sugar, star anise, cloves, cinnamon sticks, lime zest, and orange zest. Also, add the chicken bones. **(3)** Once the water starts to boil, turn down the heat to a simmer and cook for an hour with some of the lid on. **(4)** If any fat or foam comes to the surface, skim it off. **(5)** Strain the broth into a different saucepan using a fine-mesh strainer once it has simmered. Add salt to taste to season. **(6)** You may now serve the broth with the meats, pho noodles, and garnishes of your choosing.

HERBAL VEGETABLE BROTH

Preparation Time: 15 minutes || Cooking Time: 45 minutes || Servings: 4

Ingredients:

- 8 cups water
- 2 carrots, chopped
- 2 stalks celery, chopped
- 1 onion, peeled and quartered
- 1 chopped leek, just the white and light green bits
- 1 small bunch parsley
- 1 teaspoon coriander seeds
- 1 teaspoon fennel seeds
- 2 bay leaves
- 1 piece of kombu (seaweed), optional
- Salt and pepper, to taste

Instructions:

(1) In a big saucepan, combine all ingredients and bring to a boil. **(2)** On low heat, let it simmer for 45 minutes with the lid only partially on top. **(3)** Using a fine mesh strainer, transfer the broth to another saucepan. To taste, add salt and pepper for seasoning. **(4)** You may use the broth right away or keep it in the fridge for up to five days.

BEEF BONE MARROW BROTH

Preparation Time: 20 minutes || Cooking Time: 8-10 hours || Servings: 6-8

Ingredients:

4 lbs beef bones (marrow bones, knuckles, and/or oxtail)	12 cups water
2 tablespoons apple cider vinegar	1 large onion, peeled and quartered
2 carrots, chopped	2 stalks celery, chopped
1 tablespoon black peppercorns	2 bay leaves
Salt, to taste	

Instructions:

(1) Turn the oven on to 400°F or 200°C. The beef bones should be browned after 30 minutes of roasting on a baking sheet. **(2)** After transferring the roasted bones to a big saucepan, mix with apple cider vinegar and water. Give it a half-hour to sit. **(3)** To the saucepan, add the onion, carrots, celery, bay leaves, and peppercorns. Heat till boiling. **(4)** Simmer for eight to ten hours while covered and on the lowest possible heat. The broth will get richer the longer it boils. **(5)** Skim off any fat and froth that comes to the top from time to time. **(6)** Strain the broth into a different saucepan using a fine-mesh strainer once it has simmered. Add salt to taste to season. **(7)** Enjoy the broth on its own or use it as a foundation for soups like pho.

SMOKY MUSHROOM BROTH

Preparation Time: 15 minutes || Cooking Time: 1 hour || Servings: 4 servings

Ingredients:

2 tablespoons olive oil	1 large onion, sliced
4 cloves garlic, minced	1-pound mixed mushrooms (e.g., shiitake, portobello, cremini), roughly chopped
2 tablespoons soy sauce	1 teaspoon smoked paprika
8 cups vegetable broth	2 bay leaves
Salt and pepper to taste	Fresh thyme for garnish

Instructions:

(1) A big saucepan filled with olive oil should be heated over medium heat. To make the garlic and onion soft and translucent, cook them for about 5 minutes. **(2)** Simmer the mushrooms for 10 minutes until they release moisture and color. **(3)** Cover the mushrooms evenly by stirring in the smoky paprika and soy sauce. **(4)** After adding the bay leaves, pour in the vegetable broth. Heat through to a simmer. **(5)** To allow the flavors to mingle, lower the heat to low and simmer the broth, uncovered, for around 45 minutes. **(6)** To taste, add salt and pepper for seasoning. Take out the bay leaves. **(7)** Garnish with fresh thyme and serve hot.

FISH SAUCE INFUSED BROTH

Preparation Time: 10 minutes || Cooking Time: 1 hour || Servings: 4 servings

Ingredients:

2 tablespoons vegetable oil	1 large onion, quartered
4 cloves garlic, smashed	1 thumb-sized piece of ginger, sliced
8 cups chicken or vegetable broth	3 tablespoons fish sauce
1-star anise	1 cinnamon stick
2 whole cloves	Salt and pepper to taste
Fresh cilantro for garnish	

Instructions:

(1) In a big saucepan, warm the vegetable oil over medium heat. Add the ginger, garlic, and onion and sauté for 3 minutes or until fragrant. **(2)** Add the broth and mix in the cloves, cinnamon stick, star anise, and fish sauce. **(3)** After bringing the mixture to a simmer, turn down the heat. **(4)** To bring out the flavors, simmer the stock, uncovered, for approximately one hour. **(5)** To taste, add salt and pepper for seasoning. Take off the cloves, cinnamon stick, and star anise. **(6)** Garnish with fresh cilantro and serve hot.

RED CURRY COCONUT BROTH

Preparation Time: 15 minutes || Cooking Time: 30 minutes || Servings: 4 servings

Ingredients:

1 tablespoon coconut oil	2 tablespoons red curry paste
1 can (14 ounces) coconut milk	6 cups vegetable broth
1 tablespoon fish sauce (optional)	1 tablespoon brown sugar
1 stalk lemongrass, bruised	1 lime, juiced
Salt to taste	Fresh basil leaves for garnish

Instructions:

(1) In a big saucepan, warm the coconut oil over medium heat. When aromatic, add the red curry paste and sauté for one to two minutes. **(2)** Add the brown sugar, coconut milk, vegetable broth, and fish sauce (if using). Mix well to blend. **(3)** Include the bruised stalk of lemongrass. Simmer the broth for a while. **(4)** After lowering the heat to low, simmer the soup for around twenty-five minutes. **(5)** Take off the lemongrass stalk. Add salt and lime juice to taste. **(6)** Hot, garnished with basil leaves.

PHO BROTH WITH CINNAMON STICKS

Preparation Time: 30 minutes || Cooking Time: 6 hours || Servings: 6-8

Ingredients:

5 lbs beef bones (preferably marrow and knuckle bones)	1 large onion, halved and unpeeled
1 4-inch piece of ginger, halved lengthwise	5-star anise
1 cinnamon stick	3 cloves
3 cardamom pods	1 tablespoon coriander seeds
1 tablespoon salt	1/4 cup fish sauce
2 tablespoons sugar	10 cups water

Instructions:

(1) 425°F (220°C) is the temperature of the furnace. Roast beef bones on a baking pan for 30 minutes until browned. **(2)** Char onion and ginger for 5 minutes over an open flame or under a broiler until slightly browned. **(3)** Add roasted bones, charred onion, and ginger to a large stockpot with 10 cups of water. **(4)** Toast star anise, cinnamon stick, cloves, cardamom pods, and coriander seeds for 3 minutes in a dry skillet over medium heat until fragrant. Put them in the pot. **(5)** Boil then simmers. Skim surface scum. Simmer for 6 hours on low heat. **(6)** Strain broth into a clean saucepan using a fine-mesh strainer. Season with salt, fish sauce, and sugar. **(7)** Choose noodles, meats, and garnishes, and serve hot.

CHICKEN FEET BROTH

Preparation Time: 20 minutes || Cooking Time: 3 hours || Servings: 4-6

Ingredients:

2 lbs chicken feet, cleaned	10 cups water
1 onion, quartered	4 cloves garlic
1-inch piece of ginger, sliced	2 carrots, chopped
2 stalks celery, chopped	1 tablespoon apple cider vinegar
Salt and pepper to taste	

Instructions:

(1) Make a big pot and add water and chicken feet to it. Reduce the heat and let it simmer after it has boiled. Remove any foam that shows up on top by skimming it off. **(2)** Add apple cider vinegar, carrots, celery, onion, garlic, and ginger. **(3)** Simmer for three hours on low heat, skimming as necessary. **(4)** Pass the broth through a sieve with a fine mesh. To taste, add salt and pepper for seasoning. **(5)** Use as a foundation for soups or a healthy beverage.

GARLIC AND ONION BROTH

Preparation Time: 15 minutes || Cooking Time: 1 hour || Servings: 4-6

Ingredients:

3 tablespoons olive oil	5 cloves garlic, minced
2 large onions, thinly sliced	8 cups vegetable or chicken stock
1 teaspoon thyme (dried or fresh)	Salt and pepper to taste

Instructions:

(1) Get the olive oil warm by heating it in a big saucepan over medium heat. It would be well to include garlic and onions. **(2)** Simmer for 10 minutes, until the onions turn clear and start to turn brown. **(3)** Thoroughly mix the thyme and water together. Turn down the heat and cook for 45 minutes after it starts to boil. **(4)** To taste, add salt and pepper for seasoning. **(5)** Use as a tasty basis for various soups and meals or served hot.

SZECHUAN PEPPERCORN BROTH

Preparation Time: 15 minutes || Cooking Time: 2 hours || Servings: 6-8 servings

Ingredients:

2 tablespoons Szechuan peppercorns	1 large onion, quartered
4 cloves garlic, smashed	2-inch piece of ginger, sliced
2-star anise	1 cinnamon stick
6 cups beef or vegetable stock	2 tablespoons soy sauce
Salt, to taste	

Instructions:

(1) Szechuan peppercorns should be fragrant after 2 minutes in a dry pan over medium heat. Try not to burn them. **(2)** Toasted peppercorns, onion, garlic, ginger, star anise, cinnamon stick, and stock should all be combined in a big saucepan. **(3)** High heat, boil, then decrease heat and simmer, half covered, for two hours. **(4)** Transfer the broth to a new saucepan by straining it through a fine-mesh strainer. To extract as much liquid as possible, press down on the solids. **(5)** Add the soy sauce, taste it, and adjust the seasoning. **(6)** Serve hot as a delicious broth for other foods or as a foundation for noodle soups.

BEEF KNUCKLE BROTH

Preparation Time: 20 minutes || Cooking Time: 4-6 hours || Servings: 6-8 servings

Ingredients:

3 pounds of beef knuckles or marrow bones	1 large onion, halved and charred
4 cloves garlic, smashed	2-inch piece of ginger, sliced and charred
2-star anise	1 cinnamon stick
6 cups water	Salt, to taste

Instructions:

(1) Start the oven at 450°F (230°C). Bake beef knuckles or marrow bones for 30 minutes until browned. **(2)** Add the water, star anise, cinnamon stick, charred onion, garlic, ginger, and roasted bones to a large saucepan. **(3)** With a partially covered saucepan, simmer for four to six hours after boiling. Remove the foam from the surface. **(4)** Transfer the broth to a new saucepan by straining it through a fine-mesh strainer. To extract as much liquid as possible, press down on the solids. **(5)** Add salt to taste to season. **(6)** Serve hot or use it as a hearty foundation for various noodle soups, such as beef pho.

LEMONGRASS COCONUT BROTH

Preparation Time: 15 minutes || Cooking Time: 1 hour || Servings: 4-6 servings

Ingredients:

2 stalks lemongrass, tough outer layers removed, thinly sliced	1 large onion, quartered
3 cloves garlic, smashed	1-inch piece of ginger, sliced
1 can (400 ml) coconut milk	4 cups vegetable stock
2 tablespoons fish sauce (optional)	1 tablespoon lime juice
Salt, to taste	

Instructions:

(1) Lemongrass, onion, garlic, ginger, coconut milk, and vegetable stock should all be combined in a big saucepan. **(2)** Turn up the heat to high and boil. Then, turn down the heat and cook for an hour with the lid partially on top. **(3)** Transfer the broth to a new saucepan by straining it through a fine-mesh strainer. To extract as much liquid as possible, press down on the solids. **(4)** If using, add lime juice, fish sauce, and salt to taste. **(5)** Serve hot as a flavorful and light broth for other foods or as a foundation for noodle soups.

SPICY BEEF PHO BROTH

Preparation Time: 30 minutes || Cooking Time: 6 hours || Servings: 6

Ingredients:

2 lbs beef bones (marrow and knuckle bones)	1 onion, halved and unpeeled
1 4-inch piece of ginger, halved lengthwise	3-star anise
2 cinnamon sticks	3 cloves
1 cardamom pod	2 tablespoons fish sauce
1 tablespoon sugar	2 teaspoons salt
2-3 whole red chili peppers (adjust to taste)	10 cups water

Instructions:

(1) Clock in 425°F (220°C) in the oven. On a baking sheet, arrange the beef bones, onion, and ginger. Roast for about 20 minutes or until browned. **(2)** Add the ginger, onion, and roasted bones to a large saucepan. Add all the chili peppers, cardamom, cloves, cinnamon sticks, star anise, and water. **(3)** Reduce heat, cover, and simmer for six hours after boiling. Remove occasional foam buildup. **(4)** Add fish sauce, sugar, and salt in the last 30 minutes. **(5)** Pour the broth into a fresh saucepan by straining it through a fine-mesh strainer. Throw away solids. **(6)** If needed, adjust the seasoning by tasting it. Warm up the food.

MISO GINGER BROTH

Preparation Time: 15 minutes || Cooking Time: 45 minutes || Servings: 4

Ingredients:

4 cups vegetable broth	2 cups water
1/4 cup miso paste	1 tablespoon grated ginger
2 garlic cloves, minced	1 tablespoon soy sauce
1 teaspoon sesame oil	2 green onions, thinly sliced
1 cup sliced mushrooms (shiitake or button)	1 carrot, thinly sliced

Instructions:

(1) Simmer the vegetable broth with water in a big saucepan. **(2)** Blend miso paste and a tiny amount of boiling broth in a small bowl until smooth. Put aside. **(3)** Toss in the minced garlic, soy sauce, sesame oil, and grated ginger. Simmer for thirty minutes or so. **(4)** To the saucepan, add the carrot, cut mushrooms, and miso mixture. Simmer for fifteen minutes more. **(5)** Garnish the broth with green onions and serve.

ROASTED VEGETABLE BROTH

Preparation Time: 20 minutes || Cooking Time: 1 hour 30 minutes || Servings: 4-6

Ingredients:

2 carrots, chopped	2 celery stalks, chopped
1 onion, quartered	1 red bell pepper, chopped
1 tomato, quartered	1 head of garlic, halved horizontally
2 tablespoons olive oil	1 teaspoon salt
1/2 teaspoon black pepper	8 cups water
2 bay leaves	1 teaspoon dried thyme

Instructions:

(1) Set oven temperature to 400°F or 200°C. Combine olive oil, salt, and pepper with carrots, celery, onion, bell pepper, tomato, and garlic. Transfer to a baking sheet. **(2)** Vegetables should be roasted for about 40 minutes or until caramelized and soft. **(3)** Place the roasted veggies in a big saucepan. Add the thyme, bay leaves, and water. **(4)** When it starts to boil, turn down the heat and let it cook for about 45 minutes. **(5)** Pour the broth into a fresh saucepan by straining it through a fine-mesh strainer. Throw away solids. **(6)** If needed, adjust the seasoning by tasting it. Serve warm or utilize it as a filler for other recipes.

BEEF SHANK BROTH

Preparation Time: 30 minutes || Cooking Time: 6 hours || Servings: 6-8

Ingredients:

2 kg beef shank with bone	6 liters water
2 large onions, unpeeled, halved	4-inch piece ginger, unpeeled, halved lengthwise
5-star anise	1 cinnamon stick
3 cloves	1 cardamom pod
2 tablespoons fish sauce	1 tablespoon salt
1 tablespoon sugar	

Instructions:

(1) Grill onions and ginger first. Char onion and ginger peels over an open flame or broiler. Adds broth depth. **(2)** In a large stockpot, boil water. Boil beef shank loudly for 10 minutes. Remove the beef shank from the water after 10 minutes and rinse under cold water. Pot-cleaning. **(3)** Refill the pot with 6 liters of water. Clean the beef shank, add charred onions, ginger, star anise, cinnamon stick, cloves, and cardamom pod. Simmer after boiling. **(4)** Simmer broth partly covered for 6 hours Remove visible foam or fat. **(5)** After 6 hours, set aside the beef shank. Eliminate particles from the broth with a fine mesh sieve. **(6)** Sprinkle fish sauce, salt, and sugar on the soup. Spice to taste. **(7)** Cut the beef shank and add it to the broth or other recipes. With noodles, herbs, and garnishes, serve the soup hot.

SHALLOT AND BAY LEAF BROTH

Preparation Time: 20 minutes || Cooking Time: 1 hour || Servings: 4-6

Ingredients:

1 tablespoon vegetable oil	8 shallots, peeled and finely sliced
3 bay leaves	2 liters of chicken or vegetable stock
1 teaspoon black peppercorns	2 tablespoons soy sauce
1 tablespoon fish sauce	Salt, to taste
1 teaspoon sugar	

Instructions:

(1) Heat vegetable oil in a big saucepan on medium. Add the sliced shallots and simmer for 5-7 minutes until golden and softened. **(2)** Toast bay leaves and black peppercorns in the kettle for 1-2 minutes till aromatic. **(3)** Add chicken or veggie stock and boil. Add salt, sugar, soy, and fish sauce. **(4)** Let the flavors blend by simmering the stock for 45–60 minutes. Skim off surface froth and oil occasionally. **(5)** To eliminate particulates, strain broth through a fine mesh strainer after simmering. **(6)** Taste and season broth as needed. Serve hot with noodles, veggies, and protein.

TOMATO-BASED BROTH

Preparation Time: 20 minutes || Cooking Time: 1 hour 30 minutes || Servings: 4-6

Ingredients:

2 tablespoons olive oil	1 large onion, chopped
3 cloves garlic, minced	4 large tomatoes, chopped
2 liters of beef or vegetable stock	2 bay leaves
1 teaspoon dried basil	1 teaspoon dried oregano
Salt and pepper, to taste	2 tablespoons tomato paste
1 teaspoon sugar	

Instructions:

(1) Heat olive oil slowly in a big saucepan. Crush garlic and cut onion. For 5 minutes, simmer until onion is clear. **(2)** Break down the tomatoes by simmering them for 5 minutes with the chopped tomatoes. **(3)** The tomato paste should be stirred in after 2 minutes. **(4)** Add beef or vegetable stock, bay leaves, dried basil, oregano, salt, pepper, and sugar. Heat to boiling, then simmer. **(5)** Simmer the stock for 1 hour to blend the flavors and soften the tomatoes. **(6)** Take out the bay leaves and mix the soup using an immersion blender. Optional: strain broth for smoothness. **(7)** Taste and season as required. Serve hot with noodles, veggies, and protein.

THAI BASIL INFUSED BROTH

Preparation Time: 15 minutes || Cooking Time: 1 hour || Servings: 4-6

Ingredients:

2 liters of water	1 large onion, halved and charred
4 cloves of garlic, charred	1 ginger root (about 4 inches), charred
2-star anise	1 cinnamon stick
4 cardamom pods	2 tablespoons fish sauce
1 tablespoon sugar	1 cup Thai basil leaves
Salt, to taste	

Instructions:

(1) Heat the water in a big saucepan until it boils. **(2)** Toss in the cardamom pods, star anise, cinnamon stick, and caramelized onion, along with the garlic and ginger. **(3)** Reduce the heat to a simmer and let the broth steep with the spices for forty-five minutes. **(4)** Add the sugar and fish sauce, then taste and adjust the seasoning with salt. **(5)** Simmer for a further fifteen minutes after adding the Thai basil leaves. **(6)** Remove the particles from the broth by straining it through a fine strainer. **(7)** Serve hot, preferably as a foundation for your preferred noodles, meats, and garnishes for pho.

FENNEL SEED BROTH

Preparation Time: 10 minutes || Cooking Time: 1 hour 15 minutes || Servings: 4-6

Ingredients:

2 liters of water	1 large onion, halved and charred
4 cloves of garlic, charred	1 fennel bulb, chopped and charred
2 teaspoons fennel seeds	1 teaspoon coriander seeds
1 teaspoon black peppercorns	2 bay leaves
2 tablespoons soy sauce	1 tablespoon sugar
Salt, to taste	

Instructions:

(1) In a big saucepan, bring the water to a boil. **(2)** Add the bay leaves, black peppercorns, fennel seeds, roasted onion, garlic, and fennel bulb. **(3)** Turn down the heat and let it cook for an hour so that the tastes can blend. **(4)** Add sugar and soy sauce, then taste and adjust the salt. **(5)** Discard the particles after straining the broth. **(6)** Now that the broth is prepared, you may use it as a foundation for pho or other noodle soups and serve it with the sides of your choice.

ROASTED CHICKEN BONE BROTH

Preparation Time: 20 minutes (plus time for roasting bones) || Cooking Time: 3 hours || Servings: 4-6

Ingredients:

1.5 kg chicken bones, roasted	2 liters of water
1 large onion, halved and charred	4 cloves of garlic, charred
1 ginger root (about 4 inches), charred	3-star anise
2 cinnamon sticks	5 cloves
1 tablespoon apple cider vinegar	2 tablespoons fish sauce
1 tablespoon sugar	Salt, to taste

Instructions:

(1) Precondition the oven to 400°F (200°C). Spread chicken bones on a baking pan and roast until golden brown, 30–40 minutes. **(2)** Roasted chicken bones, water, charred onion, garlic, and ginger should all be combined in a big saucepan. **(3)** Toss in the cloves, cinnamon sticks, star anise, and apple cider vinegar. **(4)** Lower heat to simmer after boiling. Scrape foam from the top after three hours of lidding. **(5)** Add sugar and fish sauce, taste, and adjust the salt. **(6)** Remove the particles from the broth by straining it through a fine strainer. **(7)** When you add noodles, chicken pieces, and fresh herbs to your Roasted Chicken Bone Broth, it becomes a delicious and nutritious basis for pho.

LEMONGRASS TOFU BROTH

Preparation Time: 15 minutes || Cooking Time: 30 minutes || Servings: 4 servings

Ingredients:

6 cups vegetable stock	1 firm tofu block, diced
2 stalks lemongrass, bruised and chopped into 2-inch pieces	1 onion, halved and thinly sliced
2 cloves garlic, minced	1-inch piece ginger, sliced
2 tablespoons soy sauce	1 tablespoon vegetable oil
Salt and pepper to taste	Fresh cilantro and sliced green onions

Instructions:

(1) In a big saucepan, heat vegetable oil on medium. Sauté the sliced onion, garlic, and ginger for 5 minutes until transparent. **(2)** Sauté lemongrass for 2 minutes to unleash its scent. **(3)** Before boiling, add the vegetable stock and soy sauce. To enhance the broth's taste, simmer, covered, over low heat for 20 minutes. **(4)** Meanwhile, lightly pan-fry tofu cubes till golden brown in a separate pan. Set aside. **(5)** Strain the simmering liquid to remove lemongrass, ginger, and any solids, returning the clear broth to the saucepan. **(6)** Put pan-fried tofu in the soup. Add salt and pepper to taste. Simmer another 5 minutes. **(7)** Add chopped cilantro and green onions before serving.

PEPPERCORN CHICKEN BROTH

Preparation Time: 20 minutes || Cooking Time: 1 hour || Servings: 4 servings

Ingredients:

6 cups chicken stock	1 lb chicken breasts or thighs, skinless and boneless
1 tablespoon whole black peppercorns	1 onion, quartered
2 cloves garlic, whole	1-inch piece ginger, sliced
2 bay leaves	Salt to taste
Fresh herbs (cilantro, basil) for garnish	Lime wedges for serving

Instructions:

(1) In a large saucepan, add chicken stock, whole black peppercorns, onion, garlic, ginger, and bay leaves. Boil on medium-high. **(2)** Lower the heat and add chicken breasts or thighs to boiling water. Chicken cooks for 30 minutes under cover. **(3)** Shred the chicken into bite-sized pieces after removing it from the soup and cooling. Set aside. **(4)** Strain the soup to discard peppercorns, onion, garlic, ginger, and bay leaves. Return clear broth to pot. **(5)** Return the shredded chicken to the broth. Add salt to taste. Simmer for another 10 minutes. **(6)** Top with fresh herbs and lime wedges and serve hot.

SEAWEED AND MUSHROOM BROTH

Preparation Time: 15 minutes || Cooking Time: 25 minutes || Servings: 4 servings

Ingredients:

6 cups vegetable stock	1 cup dried seaweed (such as wakame or kombu), rinsed and soaked
1 cup mixed mushrooms (shiitake, oyster, enoki), sliced	1 onion, halved and thinly sliced
2 cloves garlic, minced	1-inch piece ginger, sliced
2 tablespoons soy sauce	1 tablespoon sesame oil
Salt and pepper to taste	Green onions and sesame seeds for garnish

Instructions:

(1) Heat sesame oil in a big saucepan on medium. Sauté the onion, garlic, and ginger for 5 minutes to soften the onion. **(2)** The mushrooms should soften after 5 minutes of sautéing. **(3)** Put in vegetable stock and soy sauce. Boil the mixture, then lower the heat. **(4)** Put the soaking seaweed in the saucepan. Simmer for 15 minutes to blend flavors. **(5)** Salt and pepper the soup to taste. **(6)** Put green onions and sesame seeds on top and serve hot.

CILANTRO LIME BROTH

Preparation Time: 10 minutes || Cooking Time: 30 minutes || Servings: 4

Ingredients:

8 cups vegetable broth	1 bunch fresh cilantro, washed and chopped
4 cloves garlic, minced	2 tablespoons grated ginger
2 stalks lemongrass, bruised and chopped	2 tablespoons soy sauce
1 tablespoon lime juice	Salt and pepper to taste

Instructions:

(1) The vegetable broth should be simmered over medium heat in a large saucepan. **(2)** Toss in the chopped lemongrass, grated ginger, minced garlic, and chopped cilantro. **(3)** Add lime juice and soy sauce and stir. **(4)** Give the broth a boil for twenty to twenty-five minutes so that the flavors may combine. **(5)** To taste, add salt and pepper for seasoning. **(6)** When the broth is finished, strain it using cheesecloth or a fine-mesh screen to get rid of any particles. **(7)** Serve hot as a foundation for pho or savor as a tasty stand-alone soup.

SHIITAKE GINGER BROTH

Preparation Time: 15 minutes || Cooking Time: 35 minutes || Servings: 4

Ingredients:

8 cups vegetable broth	1 cup dried shiitake mushrooms
4 cloves garlic, minced	2 tablespoons grated ginger
1 onion, sliced	2 tablespoons soy sauce
1 teaspoon sesame oil	Salt and pepper to taste

Instructions:

(1) On medium-high heat, bring a large saucepan of vegetable broth to a boil. **(2)** Reduce the heat to simmer after adding the dried shiitake mushrooms to the saucepan. **(3)** Add the sesame oil, soy sauce, chopped onion, grated ginger, and minced garlic. **(4)** Boil the broth for 30 minutes to infuse flavors. **(5)** To taste, add salt and pepper for seasoning. **(6)** When the broth is finished, strain it using cheesecloth or a fine-mesh screen to get rid of any particles. **(7)** Use as a savory soup base or serve hot as the foundation for pho.

COCONUT CURRY BROTH

Preparation Time: 20 minutes || Cooking Time: 40 minutes || Servings: 4

Ingredients:

2 cans (13.5 oz each) coconut milk	4 cups vegetable broth
3 tablespoons Thai red curry paste	2 tablespoons soy sauce
2 tablespoons brown sugar	1 tablespoon lime juice
1 tablespoon grated ginger	Salt to taste

Instructions:

(1) Put the vegetable broth and coconut milk in a big saucepan and heat it at a medium temperature. **(2)** Add the soy sauce, brown sugar, lime juice, grated ginger, and Thai red curry paste. **(3)** After bringing the mixture to a simmer, cook it for around 30 to 35 minutes, stirring now and again. **(4)** If necessary, taste and add more salt to the seasoning. **(5)** When the broth is finished, strain it using cheesecloth or a fine-mesh screen to get rid of any particles. **(6)** Serve hot as a foundation for pho or as a tasty soup base topped with your own ingredients.

CHAPTER: 2 BEEF PHO VARIATIONS:

TRADITIONAL BEEF PHO (PHO BO)

Preparation Time: 30 minutes || Cooking Time: 2 hours || Servings: 4-6

Ingredients:

2 onions, peeled and halved	4-inch piece of ginger, halved lengthwise
5–6-star anise	4 cloves
1 cinnamon stick	1 lb beef bones
1 lb beef brisket	6 cups of water
2 tablespoons fish sauce	Salt, to taste
1 lb rice noodles, cooked as directed	Garnish: sliced onions, chopped cilantro, bean sprouts, lime wedges, sliced chili, and fresh basil leaves

Instructions:

(1) Using a gas range or grill, softly cook the onions and ginger until they become black. This gives the broth a smokey taste. **(2)** Dry roast the cinnamon stick, cloves, and star anise in a big saucepan until aromatic. **(3)** Add 6 cups water, meat bones, brisket, ginger, and burned onions. After boiling, reduce the heat and simmer. Remove surface foam. **(4)** The brisket should be taken out after an hour, thinly sliced, and placed aside. Simmer the soup for a further hour. **(5)** After straining, pour the broth back into the pot. Add salt and fish sauce to taste. **(6)** Spoon cooked noodles into dishes to serve. Place pieces of cooked brisket on top, then cover with the heated broth. Garnishes are served on the side.

BEEF MEATBALL PHO (PHO BO VIEN)

Preparation Time: 30 minutes || Cooking Time: 2 hours || Servings: 4

Ingredients:

2 liters of beef broth	2 cinnamon sticks
3-star anise	3 cloves
1 cardamom pod	1 medium onion, charred
4-inch piece of ginger, charred	2 tablespoons fish sauce
1 tablespoon sugar	1 teaspoon salt
200g rice noodles	300g beef meatballs
Fresh herbs (cilantro, basil)	Bean sprouts, lime wedges, and sliced chili for garnish

Instructions:

(1) The beef broth should be brought to a boil in a big saucepan. Add the ginger, cloves, cinnamon sticks, star anise, cardamom pod, and charred onion. To infuse flavors, reduce heat and simmer for one and a half hours. **(2)** After straining, pour the broth back into the pot. Add salt, sugar, and fish sauce and stir. Taste and adjust the seasoning. **(3)** Pour boxed rice noodles into dishes. **(4)** Add the beef meatballs and bring the liquid to a boil. Simmer for 5 minutes or until meatballs are well heated. **(5)** Over the noodles, pour the heated broth and meatballs. Add bean sprouts, sliced Chile, lime wedges, and fresh herbs as garnish. **(6)** Enjoy your Beef Meatball Pho while it's still hot.

BEEF TENDON PHO (PHO GAN)

Preparation Time: 1 hour (plus overnight soaking for tendons) || Cooking Time: 4 hours || Servings: 4

Ingredients:

2 liters of beef broth	500g beef tendons
2 cinnamon sticks	3-star anise
3 cloves	1 cardamom pod
1 medium onion, charred	4-inch piece of ginger, charred
2 tablespoons fish sauce	1 tablespoon sugar
1 teaspoon salt	200g rice noodles
Fresh herbs (cilantro, basil)	Bean sprouts, lime wedges, and sliced chili for garnish

Instructions:

(1) Overnight, soak beef tendons in cold water. **(2)** Tendons are drained and put in a pot. Bring the water to a boil while covering. After ten minutes of simmering, strain and rinse. **(3)** Sanitize a saucepan and boil beef broth. Stir in ginger, charred onion, cloves, cardamom, cinnamon, star anise, and precooked tendons. Simmer for 3–4 hours to soften tendons. **(4)** Cut out the tendons, thinly slice, and put aside. After straining, pour the broth back into the pot. Add salt, sugar, and fish sauce and stir. **(5)** Pour the rice noodles onto serving bowls after cooking them as recommended on the box. **(6)** Spoon cut tendrils into each dish. Cover noodles and tendons with heated broth. Add bean sprouts, sliced Chile, lime wedges, and fresh herbs as garnish. **(7)** Serve heated Pho with Beef Tendon.

BEEF TRIPE PHO (PHO SACH)

Preparation Time: 30 minutes || Cooking Time: 2 hours || Servings: 4

Ingredients:

2 liters of beef broth	300g beef tripe, thinly sliced
2 cinnamon sticks	3-star anise
3 cloves	1 cardamom pod
1 medium onion, charred	4-inch piece of ginger, charred
2 tablespoons fish sauce	1 tablespoon sugar
1 teaspoon salt	200g rice noodles
Fresh herbs (cilantro, basil)	Bean sprouts, lime wedges, and sliced chili for garnish

Instructions:

(1) The beef broth should be brought to a boil in a big saucepan. Add the ginger, cloves, cinnamon sticks, star anise, cardamom pod, and charred onion. To infuse flavors, reduce heat and simmer for one and a half hours. **(2)** After straining, pour the broth back into the pot. Add salt, sugar, and fish sauce and stir. Taste and adjust the seasoning. **(3)** Pour boxed rice noodles into dishes. **(4)** Add the thinly sliced beef tripe to the boiling stock. Cook until tripe is tender, about 10 minutes. **(5)** Over the noodles, pour the boiling broth and tripe. Add bean sprouts, sliced Chile, lime wedges, and fresh herbs as garnish. **(6)** Enjoy your hot beef tripe soup after serving!

BEEF FLANK PHO (PHO NAM)

Preparation Time: 30 minutes || Cooking Time: 2 hours || Servings: 4

Ingredients:

1 lb. beef flank, thinly sliced	8 cups beef broth
1 onion, halved and charred	4-inch piece of ginger, halved and charred
2 cinnamon sticks	4-star anise
4 cloves	2 cardamom pods
2 tablespoons fish	Salt, to taste

sauce
Rice noodles, as needed

Garnishes: bean sprouts, sliced onions, cilantro, lime wedges, sliced jalapeños, hoisin sauce, Sriracha

Instructions:

(1) Boil beef broth in a big pot. Use cardamom, cloves, star anise, charred onion, ginger, and cinnamon sticks. Simmer on low for 1.5 hours to create flavors. **(2)** Add salt and fish sauce to flavor the soup. To get rid of solids and spices, strain. **(3)** Prepare rice noodles according to the packet. **(4)** Divide the noodles among bowls. Top with a thinly sliced beef flank. **(5)** Cover the noodles and meat with heated broth. The meat will be cooked by the broth's heat. **(6)** Present it with garnishes so that guests can customize it to their taste.

BEEF SHANK PHO (PHO GAU)

Preparation Time: 30 minutes || Cooking Time: 2.5 hours || Servings: 4

Ingredients:

1 lb beef shank, cut into chunks	8 cups beef broth
1 onion, halved and charred	4-inch piece of ginger, halved and charred
3 cinnamon sticks	5-star anise
5 cloves	3 cardamom pods
2 tablespoons fish sauce	Salt, to taste
Rice noodles, as needed	Garnishes: bean sprouts, sliced onions, cilantro, lime wedges, sliced jalapeños, hoisin sauce, Sriracha

Instructions:

(1) Simmer the beef shank for two hours or until the meat is cooked in a large saucepan with charred onion, ginger, cinnamon sticks, star anise, cloves, and cardamom pods in beef broth. **(2)** Take off the beef shank, cut it thinly, and put it aside. **(3)** Strain the soup, then add salt and fish sauce for seasoning. **(4)** Prepare rice noodles according to the packet. **(5)** In bowls, arrange noodles and sliced beef shank. **(6)** Cover the noodles and meat with heated broth. **(7)** Garnish and serve.

SPICY BEEF PHO

Preparation Time: 30 minutes || Cooking Time: 2 hours || Servings: 4

Ingredients:

1 lb beef sirloin, thinly sliced	8 cups beef broth
1 onion, halved and charred	4-inch piece of ginger, halved and charred
2 cinnamon sticks	4-star anise
4 cloves	2 cardamom pods
3 tablespoons fish sauce	2 tablespoons chili paste (adjust to taste)
Salt, to taste	Rice noodles, as needed
Garnishes: bean sprouts, sliced onions, cilantro, lime wedges, sliced jalapeños, hoisin sauce, Sriracha	

Instructions:

(1) Boil beef broth in a big pot. Use cardamom, cloves, star anise, charred onion, ginger, and cinnamon sticks. Simmer 1.5 hours. **(2)** Add the salt, chili paste, and fish sauce to taste. **(3)** To get rid of the sediments and spices, strain the broth. **(4)** Make rice noodles according to the directions on the box. **(5)** Fill dishes with noodles with thinly sliced steak sirloin. **(6)** Cook the beef slices by pouring boiling broth over the steak and noodles. **(7)** Serve garnished for more spiciness and taste.

LEMONGRASS BEEF PHO

Preparation Time: 30 minutes || Cooking Time: 2 hours || Servings: 4

Ingredients:

1 pound beef sirloin, thinly sliced	8 cups beef broth
2 stalks lemongrass,	3 shallots, sliced

bruised and chopped	
3 cloves garlic, minced	1 tablespoon ginger, grated
2 tablespoons fish sauce	1 tablespoon sugar
1 cinnamon stick	4-star anise
6 cloves	8 ounces dried rice noodles
1 cup bean sprouts	1/2 cup fresh basil leaves
1/2 cup cilantro leaves	1 lime, cut into wedges
Sriracha sauce (optional)	Hoisin sauce (optional)

Instructions:

(1) In a large saucepan, add beef broth, lemongrass, shallots, garlic, ginger, fish sauce, sugar, cinnamon stick, star anise, and cloves. Turn down the heat and let it cook for an hour after it boils. **(2)** While the broth simmers, cook the rice noodles per the box. Drain and set aside. **(3)** Return the broth to the pot after straining. Return to simmer. **(4)** Cook the sliced beef in the boiling liquid for 2-3 minutes until just done. **(5)** Divide cooked noodles into bowls to serve. Cover noodles with heated broth and meat. Add bean sprouts, basil, cilantro, and lime juice. If preferred, serve with sriracha and hoisin sauce.

BLACK PEPPER BEEF PHO

Preparation Time: 20 minutes || Cooking Time: 1 hour 30 minutes || Servings: 4

Ingredients:

1 pound beef brisket, sliced thinly	8 cups beef broth
1 onion, sliced	4 cloves garlic, minced
2 tablespoons black peppercorns, crushed	2 tablespoons fish sauce
1 tablespoon sugar	1 cinnamon stick
4-star anise	8 ounces dried rice noodles
1 cup bean sprouts	1/2 cup Thai basil leaves
1/2 cup cilantro leaves	1 lime, cut into wedges

Instructions:

(1) In a big saucepan, add beef broth, onion, garlic, black peppercorns, fish sauce, sugar, cinnamon stick, and star anise. Turn down the heat and let it cook for an hour after it boils. **(2)** While the broth simmers, cook the rice noodles per the box. Drain and set aside. **(3)** Return the broth to the pot after straining. Return to simmer. **(4)** Cook the sliced beef brisket in the boiling stock for 10-15 minutes until tender. **(5)** Divide cooked noodles into bowls to serve. Cover noodles with heated broth and meat. Add bean sprouts, Thai basil, cilantro, and lime juice.

FIVE-SPICE BEEF PHO

Preparation Time: 40 minutes || Cooking Time: 2 hours 15 minutes || Servings: 4

Ingredients:

1 pound beef round, thinly sliced	8 cups beef broth
1 onion, sliced	4 cloves garlic, minced
2 tablespoons five-spice powder	2 tablespoons fish sauce
1 tablespoon sugar	1 cinnamon stick
4-star anise	8 ounces dried rice noodles
1 cup bean sprouts	1/2 cup mint leaves
1/2 cup cilantro leaves	1 lime, cut into wedges

Instructions:

(1) Mix fish sauce, sugar, cinnamon stick, star anise, onion, garlic, five-spice powder, and sugar in a large pot. Lower the heat and simmer for two hours after boiling. **(2)** Cook the rice noodles per the box while the broth boils. Remove after draining. **(3)** After straining the broth to get rid of the solids, put it back in the saucepan. Return it to a simmer. **(4)** After the stock boils, add the sliced beef round and simmer for two to three minutes until just done. **(5)** The cooked noodles should be divided into serving dishes for serving. Over the noodles, ladle the boiling soup and steak. Add bean sprouts, cilantro, mint, and a squeeze of lime juice on top.

GARLIC BEEF PHO

Preparation Time: 30 minutes || Cooking Time: 2 hours || Servings: 4

Ingredients:

1 lb beef bones	1 lb beef brisket
8 cups water	1 onion, peeled and halved
4 cloves of garlic, minced	1 ginger piece (2 inches), peeled and halved
2-star anise	1 cinnamon stick
2 cloves	1 teaspoon salt
2 tablespoons fish sauce	200g rice noodles
1 cup bean sprouts	Fresh herbs (basil, cilantro, mint)
Lime wedges for serving	Hoisin sauce and Sriracha for serving

Instructions:

(1) Put the brisket, water, and beef bones into a big saucepan. Bring to a boil, making sure to skim off any froth that rises to the top. **(2)** Add the onion, cloves, cinnamon, ginger, star anise, and reduce heat to a simmer. The brisket should be tender after 1.5 hours of simmering under cover. **(3)** After removing the brisket, leave it to cool. Cut thinly. **(4)** After straining, put the broth back in the pot. Add fish sauce and salt for seasoning. **(5)** As directed on the package, prepare the rice noodles. **(6)** Divide the noodles among dishes for serving. Add fresh herbs, bean sprouts, and beef pieces on top. **(7)** Ladle hot broth on top. Present the dish alongside lime wedges, hoisin sauce, and Sriracha.

SATAY BEEF PHO

Preparation Time: 30 minutes || Cooking Time: 2 hours || Servings: 4

Ingredients:

1 lb beef bones	1 lb beef sirloin, thinly sliced
8 cups water	1 onion, peeled and halved
1 ginger piece (2 inches), peeled and halved	2 tablespoons peanut butter
2 tablespoons soy sauce	1 tablespoon chili paste
1 teaspoon curry powder	2-star anise
1 cinnamon stick	200g rice noodles
1 cup bean sprouts	Fresh herbs (basil, cilantro, mint)
Lime wedges for serving	Hoisin sauce and Sriracha for serving

Instructions:

(1) In a big pot, put the pork bones and water. Bring it to a boil, then turn down the heat so it simmers. **(2)** Combine peanut butter, soy sauce, curry powder, and chili paste in another bowl. Combine this blend with the onion, ginger, star anise, and cinnamon stick in the saucepan. Simmer for one and a half hours. **(3)** Prepare rice noodles according to the packet. **(4)** Before serving, add thinly sliced beef sirloin to the stew. Cook until barely done, 1–2 minutes. **(5)** Divide the noodles among dishes for serving. Add bean sprouts, fresh herbs, and slices of meat on top. **(6)** Ladle hot broth on top. Present the dish alongside lime wedges, hoisin sauce, and Sriracha.

GINGER BEEF PHO

Preparation Time: 30 minutes || Cooking Time: 2 hours || Servings: 4

Ingredients:

1 lb beef bones	1 lb beef tenderloin, thinly sliced
8 cups water	1 large onion, peeled and halved
4 inches fresh ginger, peeled and sliced	2-star anise
1 cinnamon stick	4 cardamom pods
1 teaspoon salt	2 tablespoons fish

200g rice noodles	sauce
Fresh herbs (basil, cilantro, mint)	1 cup bean sprouts
Hoisin sauce and Sriracha for serving	Lime wedges for serving

Instructions:

(1) Add the water and the meat bones to a large saucepan. Reduce the heat to low and simmer after it has boiled. **(2)** Stir in the cardamom pods, cinnamon, star anise, onion, and ginger. Simmer for one and a half hours. **(3)** After taking out the meat bones, drain the broth. Put the soup back in the pot and add fish sauce and salt to taste. **(4)** As directed on the package, prepare the rice noodles. **(5)** Add the thinly sliced beef tenderloin to the stew right before serving. Cook for one to two minutes or until just done. **(6)** Divide the noodles among dishes for serving. Add bean sprouts, fresh herbs, and slices of meat on top. **(7)** Ladle hot broth on top. Present the dish alongside lime wedges, hoisin sauce, and Sriracha.

COCONUT BEEF PHO

Preparation Time: 30 minutes || Cooking Time: 2 hours || Servings: 4

Ingredients:

1 lb beef brisket	4 cups beef broth
2 cups coconut milk	1 onion, sliced
4 cloves garlic, minced	2-inch piece ginger, sliced
2-star anise	1 cinnamon stick
2 tablespoons fish sauce	Salt and pepper, to taste
200g rice noodles	1 lime, cut into wedges
Fresh cilantro, basil, and mint for garnish	Bean sprouts, for garnish
2 jalapeños, sliced, for garnish	

Instructions:

(1) Beef brisket, beef broth, coconut milk, star anise, onion, garlic, ginger, and cinnamon stick should all be combined in a big saucepan. When the meat is tender, simmer it for one and a half to two hours over low heat after bringing it to a boil. **(2)** After taking the meat out of the liquid, thinly slice it. After straining, pour the broth back into the pot. Add salt, pepper, and fish sauce for seasoning. **(3)** As directed on the package, prepare the rice noodles. **(4)** Divide the noodles among dishes for serving. Place the sliced meat on top, then pour the heated broth over the noodles and steak. **(5)** Add bean sprouts, jalapeños, fresh herbs, and lime wedges as garnish. Serve right away.

HOISIN BEEF PHO

Preparation Time: 20 minutes || Cooking Time: 2 hours || Servings: 4

Ingredients:

1 lb beef sirloin, thinly sliced	4 cups beef broth
1 onion, charred	4 cloves garlic, minced
2-inch piece ginger, charred	1 cinnamon stick
3-star anise	1/4 cup hoisin sauce
2 tablespoons soy sauce	200g rice noodles
Fresh cilantro for garnish	Green onions, sliced, for garnish
Lime wedges for serving	Bean sprouts, for garnish

Instructions:

(1) Place the charred onion, ginger, garlic, star anise, cinnamon stick, and beef broth in a large pot. After boiling, reduce heat and simmer for 1.5 hours. **(2)** To the broth, add the soy sauce and hoisin sauce. After giving it a good stir, simmer for a further half hour. **(3)** As you wait, make the rice noodles as directed on the package. **(4)** Place the finely cut sirloin into individual dishes. The meat should be covered with the boiling broth and allowed to simmer in it. **(5)** To each bowl, add cooked rice noodles. **(6)** Bean sprouts, lime wedges, cilantro, and green onions are used as garnish. Serve right away.

SRIRACHA BEEF PHO

Preparation Time: 20 minutes || Cooking Time: 2 hours || Servings: 4

Ingredients:

1 lb beef flank, thinly sliced	4 cups beef broth
1 large onion, halved and charred	4 cloves garlic, minced
2-inch piece ginger, charred	3-star anise
1 cinnamon stick	2 tablespoons fish sauce
1-2 tablespoons Sriracha sauce, to taste	200g rice noodles
Lime wedges for serving	Fresh basil for garnish
Bean sprouts, for garnish	Sliced jalapeños for garnish

Instructions:

(1) Add the cinnamon stick, star anise, garlic, charred onion, and ginger to a large saucepan along with the beef stock. **(2)** It's best to let the tastes develop over a period of 1.5 hours after bringing the mixture to a boil. **(3)** After removing the aromatics, taste and adjust the soup with fish sauce and Sriracha sauce. **(4)** Prepare rice noodles according to the packet. **(5)** Spoon the thinly sliced flank of beef into each dish. To cook the meat, pour the boiling stock over it. **(6)** Fill each bowl with the cooked rice noodles. **(7)** Add sliced jalapeños, bean sprouts, fresh basil, and lime wedges as garnish. Warm up the food.

BASIL BEEF PHO

Preparation Time: 30 minutes || Cooking Time: 2 hours || Servings: 4

Ingredients:

2 lbs beef bones	1 onion, halved and charred
4 cloves of garlic, charred	1 ginger piece (2 inches), charred
2-star anise	1 cinnamon stick
4 cloves	4 cups beef broth
2 tbsp fish sauce	Salt, to taste
8 oz rice noodles	1 lb beef sirloin, thinly sliced
1 cup basil leaves	Bean sprouts, lime wedges, sliced chili, and hoisin sauce for serving

Instructions:

(1) Soak beef bones, charred onion, garlic, ginger, star anise, cinnamon, and cloves in beef broth for one and a half hours in a big saucepan. If any foam appears at the top, skim it off. **(2)** After straining, pour the broth back into the pot. To taste, add salt and fish sauce. Maintain its warmth on low heat. **(3)** Follow the box instructions to cook rice noodles. Divide among four servings. **(4)** Top the noodles with thinly sliced beef sirloin and basil leaves. **(5)** Make sure the steak is well cooked by covering it with the hot broth as you pour it into each bowl. **(6)** Serve right away, garnished with sliced chiles, lime wedges, bean sprouts, and hoisin sauce.

CURRY BEEF PHO

Preparation Time: 30 minutes || Cooking Time: 2 hours || Servings: 4

Ingredients:

2 lbs beef bones	1 onion, halved and charred
4 cloves of garlic, charred	1 ginger piece (2 inches), charred
1 lemongrass stalk, bruised	3 tbsp curry powder
4 cups beef broth	2 tbsp fish sauce
Salt, to taste	8 oz rice noodles
1 lb beef sirloin, thinly sliced	Cilantro and sliced green onions for garnish
Bean sprouts, lime wedges, and sliced chili for serving	

Instructions:

(1) Simmer the beef bones, curry powder, garlic, ginger, charred onion, lemongrass, and beef broth for one and a half hours in a big saucepan. Remove any froth with a skim. **(2)** After straining, pour the broth back into the pot. Add fish sauce and salt for seasoning. Maintain warmth on low heat. **(3)** After cooking the rice noodles according to the package's directions, divide them into four bowls. **(4)** Place thinly sliced beef sirloin over noodles. **(5)** Spoon the heated broth with a hint of spice over the noodles and steak. **(6)** Add green onions and cilantro as garnish. Accompany with sliced chiles, lime wedges, and bean sprouts.

KIMCHI BEEF PHO

Preparation Time: 30 minutes || Cooking Time: 2 hours || Servings: 4

Ingredients:

2 lbs beef bones	1 onion, halved and charred
4 cloves of garlic, charred	1 ginger piece (2 inches), charred
4 cups beef broth	2 tbsp fish sauce
Salt, to taste	8 oz rice noodles
1 lb beef sirloin, thinly sliced	1 cup kimchi, chopped
1 tbsp kimchi juice	Green onions and cilantro for garnish
Bean sprouts, lime wedges, and sliced chili for serving	

Instructions:

(1) Simmer the beef bones, ginger, garlic, and charred onion in beef stock for one and a half hours in a big saucepan. Take out any foam. **(2)** After straining, pour the broth back into the pot. Stir in the kimchi juice, fish sauce, and salt to taste. Maintain warmth on low heat. **(3)** After preparing the rice noodles per the directions on the package, divide them into four bowls. **(4)** Over the noodles, scatter the chopped kimchi and thinly sliced beef sirloin. **(5)** To cook the beef slices, pour the boiling stock into each dish. **(6)** Add cilantro and green onions as garnish. Accompany with sliced chiles, lime wedges, and bean sprouts.

RED WINE BEEF PHO

Preparation Time: 30 minutes || Cooking Time: 2 hours || Servings: 4

Ingredients:

2 lbs beef bones	1 onion, halved and unpeeled
1 ginger piece (about 4 inches), halved lengthwise	1 cup red wine
8 cups water	3-star anise
2 cinnamon sticks	4 cloves
2 cardamom pods	1 tablespoon salt
2 tablespoons fish sauce	1 lb beef sirloin, thinly sliced
Rice noodles (pho), as needed	Fresh herbs (cilantro, basil), bean sprouts, lime wedges, and sliced chili for garnish

Instructions:

(1) Glaze the oven at 220°C (425°F). Brown beef bones, onion, and ginger on a baking pan for 30 minutes. **(2)** Add roasted bones, onion, ginger, red wine, and water to a large saucepan. First, boil, then simmer. **(3)** Cinnamon, cloves, cardamom, and star anise. Reduce heat and cover for 1.5 hours. **(4)** Refill the pot with strained broth. Salt and fish sauce. **(5)** Prep rice noodles per packet. **(6)** Cook the thinly sliced beef sirloin for 1-2 minutes in simmering stock. **(7)** Pour steak and boiling broth over noodles in bowls. **(8)** Sides include fresh herbs, bean sprouts, lime wedges, and sliced chiles.

PINEAPPLE BEEF PHO

Preparation Time: 20 minutes || Cooking Time: 2 hours || Servings: 4

Ingredients:

2 lbs beef bones	1 onion, halved and unpeeled

1 ginger piece (about 4 inches), halved lengthwise	8 cups water
1 cup fresh pineapple, chopped	3-star anise
2 cinnamon sticks	4 cloves
1 tablespoon salt	2 tablespoons fish sauce
1 lb beef sirloin, thinly sliced	Rice noodles (pho), as needed
Fresh herbs (cilantro, basil), bean sprouts, lime wedges, and sliced chili for garnish	

Instructions:

(1) To make a flavorful broth, simmer water, onion, and beef bones in a big saucepan for two hours. **(2)** To the broth, add the pineapple, cloves, cinnamon, and star anise. Simmer for a further thirty minutes. **(3)** After straining, pour the broth back into the pot. Add fish sauce and salt for seasoning. **(4)** Follow the box instructions to cook rice noodles. **(5)** After bringing the stock to a boil and adding the thinly sliced beef sirloin, cook it for one to two minutes or until it's just done. **(6)** Spoon noodles into individual dishes, then pour heated broth and steak over them. **(7)** Accompany with sliced chiles, bean sprouts, lime wedges, and fresh herbs.

HONEY SOY BEEF PHO

Preparation Time: 20 minutes || Cooking Time: 2 hours || Servings: 4

Ingredients:

2 lbs beef bones	1 onion, halved and unpeeled
1 ginger piece (about 4 inches), halved lengthwise	8 cups water
¼ cup soy sauce	2 tablespoons honey
3-star anise	2 cinnamon sticks
4 cloves	1 tablespoon salt
2 tablespoons fish sauce	1 lb beef sirloin, thinly sliced
Rice noodles (pho), as needed	Fresh herbs (cilantro, basil), bean sprouts, lime wedges, and sliced chili for garnish

Instructions:

(1) To make a flavorful broth, simmer water, onion, and beef bones in a big saucepan for two hours. **(2)** To the broth, add cloves, cinnamon, star anise, honey, and soy sauce. Keep it simmering for half an hour more. **(3)** After straining, pour the broth back into the pot. Add fish sauce and salt for seasoning. **(4)** Follow the box instructions to cook rice noodles. **(5)** After bringing the stock to a boil and adding the thinly sliced beef sirloin, cook it for one to two minutes or until it's just done. **(6)** Spoon noodles into individual dishes, then pour heated broth and steak over them. **(7)** Accompany with sliced chiles, bean sprouts, lime wedges, and fresh herbs.

TERIYAKI BEEF PHO

Preparation Time: 20 minutes || Cooking Time: 2 hours || Servings: 4

Ingredients:

1 lb beef brisket, thinly sliced	4 cups beef broth
2 cups water	1 large onion, sliced
4 cloves garlic, minced	2-inch piece ginger, sliced
3 tablespoons teriyaki sauce	2 tablespoons soy sauce
1 tablespoon brown sugar	200g rice noodles
2 green onions, chopped	1 cup bean sprouts
Fresh cilantro for garnish	Lime wedges for serving

Instructions:

(1) Ginger, garlic, onion, and beef stock should all be combined in a big saucepan. Boil for one and a half hours, then lower the heat and simmer. **(2)** Combine brown sugar, soy sauce, and teriyaki sauce in a bowl. Slices of beef brisket should be added and marinated for at least half an hour. **(3)** After taking the brisket out of the marinade, fry it for two minutes on each side in a hot pan. Put aside. **(4)** As directed on the package, prepare the rice noodles. **(5)** Spoon some rice noodles into a dish and serve. Add bean sprouts, green onions, and pieces of meat on top. Spoon heated stock onto the noodles. Serve with lime wedges on the side and garnish with fresh cilantro.

CITRUS BEEF PHO

Preparation Time: 25 minutes || Cooking Time: 2 hours || Servings: 4

Ingredients:

1 lb beef sirloin, thinly sliced	4 cups beef broth
2 cups water	1 large onion, sliced
4 cloves garlic, minced	2-inch piece ginger, sliced
Peel of 1 orange	Juice of 1 orange
2 tablespoons fish sauce	1 tablespoon sugar
200g rice noodles	2 green onions, chopped
1 cup bean sprouts	Fresh mint, for garnish
Lime wedges for serving	

Instructions:

(1) Orange peel, onion, garlic, ginger, and beef broth should all be combined in a big saucepan. Boil for one and a half hours, then lower the heat and simmer. **(2)** Add sugar, fish sauce, and orange juice to the broth. Mix thoroughly. **(3)** After adding the beef sirloin pieces, simmer for a further ten minutes. **(4)** As directed on the package, prepare the rice noodles. **(5)** Spoon some rice noodles into a dish and serve. Add bean sprouts, green onions, and pieces of meat on top. Spoon heated stock onto the noodles. Serve with lime wedges on the side and garnish with fresh mint.

WASABI BEEF PHO

Preparation Time: 20 minutes || Cooking Time: 2 hours || Servings: 4

Ingredients:

1 lb beef tenderloin, thinly sliced	4 cups beef broth
2 cups water	1 large onion, sliced
4 cloves garlic, minced	2-inch piece ginger, sliced
1 tablespoon wasabi paste (adjust to taste)	2 tablespoons soy sauce
1 tablespoon sugar	200g rice noodles
2 green onions, chopped	1 cup bean sprouts
Fresh basil for garnish	Lime wedges for serving

Instructions:

(1) Ginger, garlic, onion, and beef stock should all be combined in a big saucepan. Boil for one and a half hours, then lower the heat and simmer. **(2)** Mix sugar, soy sauce, and wasabi paste together in a small bowl. Mix it into the water by stirring it in. **(3)** After adding the beef tenderloin pieces, simmer for a further ten minutes. **(4)** As directed on the package, prepare the rice noodles. **(5)** Spoon some rice noodles into a dish and serve. Add bean sprouts, green onions, and pieces of meat on top. Spoon heated stock onto the noodles. Serve with lime wedges on the side and garnish with fresh basil.

PESTO BEEF PHO

Preparation Time: 20 minutes || Cooking Time: 2 hours || Servings: 4

Ingredients:

1 pound beef sirloin, thinly sliced	8 cups beef broth
1 onion, sliced	3 cloves garlic, minced
1-inch ginger, sliced	2 tablespoons fish sauce
1 tablespoon soy sauce	1 tablespoon brown sugar
8 ounces rice noodles	1 cup fresh basil leaves
½ cup pine nuts	2 cloves garlic
½ cup grated Parmesan cheese	½ cup olive oil

Salt and pepper to taste	Bean sprouts, lime wedges, and jalapeño slices for serving

Instructions:

(1) The beef stock should be simmered over medium heat in a large saucepan. Add the brown sugar, fish sauce, soy sauce, onion, garlic, and ginger. Simmer it for half an hour. **(2)** As you wait, prepare the rice noodles per the directions on the box. After draining, set away. **(3)** Olive oil, Parmesan cheese, garlic, pine nuts, and basil leaves should all be combined in a blender. Process till smooth. To taste, add salt and pepper for seasoning. **(4)** When the meat is cooked through, add the sliced beef to the stock and simmer for an additional 10 to 15 minutes. **(5)** The cooked rice noodles should be divided into serving dishes. Over the noodles, ladle the beef broth. Place a dollop of pesto on top. Present bean sprouts, wedges of lime, and slices of jalapeño on the side.

CILANTRO LIME BEEF PHO

Preparation Time: 15 minutes || Cooking Time: 2 hours || Servings: 4

Ingredients:

1 pound beef flank steak, thinly sliced	8 cups beef broth
1 onion, sliced	3 cloves garlic, minced
1-inch ginger, sliced	2 tablespoons fish sauce
1 tablespoon soy sauce	1 tablespoon brown sugar
8 ounces rice noodles	1 cup fresh cilantro leaves
1 lime, sliced	2 green onions, chopped
Sriracha sauce and hoisin sauce for serving	

Instructions:

(1) The beef stock should be simmered over medium heat in a large saucepan. Add the brown sugar, fish sauce, soy sauce, onion, garlic, and ginger. Simmer it for half an hour. **(2)** As you wait, prepare the rice noodles per the directions on the box. After draining, set away. **(3)** When the meat is cooked through, add the sliced beef to the stock and simmer for an additional 10 to 15 minutes. **(4)** The cooked rice noodles should be divided into serving dishes. Over the noodles, ladle the beef broth. Add sliced limes, chopped green onions, and fresh cilantro leaves on top. Serve with Hoisin and Sriracha sauces on the side.

CHIPOTLE BEEF PHO

Preparation Time: 25 minutes || Cooking Time: 2 hours || Servings: 4

Ingredients:

1 pound beef brisket, thinly sliced	8 cups beef broth
1 onion, sliced	3 cloves garlic, minced
1-inch ginger, sliced	2 chipotle peppers in adobo sauce, chopped
2 tablespoons fish sauce	1 tablespoon soy sauce
1 tablespoon brown sugar	8 ounces rice noodles
1 cup sliced mushrooms	½ cup sliced bell peppers
Fresh cilantro leaves for garnish	Lime wedges for serving

Instructions:

(1) The beef stock should be simmered over medium heat in a large saucepan. Add the brown sugar, fish sauce, soy sauce, chipotle peppers, onion, garlic, and ginger. Simmer it for half an hour. **(2)** As you wait, prepare the rice noodles per the directions on the box. After draining, set away. **(3)** When the meat is cooked through, add the sliced beef brisket to the stock and simmer for an additional 10 to 15 minutes. **(4)** Simmer the bell peppers and sliced mushrooms in the broth for a further five minutes. **(5)** The cooked rice noodles should be divided into serving dishes. Over the noodles, ladle the beef broth. Serve with lime wedges on the side and garnish with fresh cilantro leaves.

BALSAMIC GLAZED BEEF PHO

Preparation Time: 30 minutes || Cooking Time: 2 hours || Servings: 4

Ingredients:

- 1 lb beef brisket
- 1 onion, sliced
- 1 cinnamon stick
- 1/4 cup balsamic vinegar
- 1 tbsp brown sugar
- 200g rice noodles
- 8 cups beef broth
- 4 cloves garlic, minced
- 2-star anise
- 2 tbsp soy sauce
- Salt and pepper to taste
- Garnishes: Fresh basil, bean sprouts, lime wedges, sliced chili

Instructions:

(1) Beef brisket, beef broth, onion, garlic, star anise, and cinnamon stick should all be combined in a big saucepan. **(2)** After a boil, reduce heat and simmer the meat for 1 hour. **(3)** After removing, let the beef brisket to cool. Cut thinly. **(4)** After straining, pour the broth back into the pot. Brown sugar, soy sauce, and balsamic vinegar should be added to the broth. Add pepper and salt for seasoning. Heat through to a simmer. **(5)** Cook rice noodles according to the box. **(6)** Spoon noodles into each bowl. Add sliced meat on top. Cover the noodles and meat with heated broth. **(7)** Garnishes are served on the side.

MUSTARD SEED BEEF PHO

Preparation Time: 30 minutes || Cooking Time: 2 hours || Servings: 4

Ingredients:

- 1 lb beef shank
- 1 onion, sliced
- 1 tbsp mustard seeds
- 1 cinnamon stick
- 200g rice noodles
- 8 cups beef broth
- 4 cloves garlic, minced
- 2 bay leaves
- Salt and pepper to taste
- Garnishes: Fresh cilantro, sliced green onions, lime wedges, jalapeño slices

Instructions:

(1) Toast mustard seeds until they explode on a dry pan. Take out and set aside. **(2)** Beef shank, beef broth, onion, garlic, roasted mustard seeds, bay leaves, and cinnamon sticks should all be combined in a big saucepan. **(3)** To tenderize the beef, decrease the heat and simmer for two hours after boiling. **(4)** Take out the beef shank, allow it to cool, and then thinly slice. **(5)** After straining, pour the broth back into the pot. Add pepper and salt for seasoning. Heat through to a simmer. **(6)** Cook rice noodles according to the box. **(7)** Spoon noodles into each bowl. Add sliced meat on top. Cover the noodles and meat with heated broth. **(8)** Garnishes are served on the side.

SZECHUAN BEEF PHO

Preparation Time: 30 minutes || Cooking Time: 2 hours || Servings: 4

Ingredients:

- 1 lb beef sirloin
- 1 onion, sliced
- 1 tbsp Szechuan peppercorns
- 1 cinnamon stick
- Salt to taste
- Garnishes: Fresh mint, bean sprouts, lime wedges, thinly sliced red chili
- 8 cups beef broth
- 4 cloves garlic, minced
- 2-star anise
- 2 tbsp chili oil
- 200g rice noodles

Instructions:

(1) Beef sirloin, beef broth, onion, garlic, Szechuan peppercorns, star anise, and cinnamon stick should all be combined in a big saucepan. **(2)** To tenderize the beef, decrease the heat and simmer for two hours after boiling. **(3)** Take out the beef sirloin, let it cool, and then thinly slice. **(4)** After straining, pour the broth back into the pot. Add salt to taste and Chile oil. Heat through to a simmer. **(5)** Cook rice noodles according to the box. **(6)** Spoon noodles into each bowl. Add sliced meat on top. Cover the noodles and meat with heated broth. **(7)** Garnishes are served on the side.

MANGO BEEF PHO

Preparation Time: 20 minutes || Cooking Time: 2 hours || Servings: 4

Ingredients:

8 cups beef broth	1 lb beef sirloin, thinly sliced
2 ripe mangoes, peeled and diced	1 onion, thinly sliced
3 cloves garlic, minced	1 tablespoon ginger, grated
2 tablespoons fish sauce	1 tablespoon soy sauce
1 tablespoon brown sugar	8 oz rice noodles
Fresh cilantro leaves, bean sprouts, lime wedges for garnish	

Instructions:

(1) Simmer the beef stock in a large saucepan over medium heat. **(2)** To the saucepan, add the sliced meat, onion, garlic, ginger, soy sauce, fish sauce, and brown sugar. Mix everything together. **(3)** Simmer the stock for one and a half to two hours or until the meat is very soft and the flavors are thoroughly combined. **(4)** While waiting, cook and drain the rice noodles according to the instructions. **(5)** Add the diced mangoes to the saucepan and cook for an additional five minutes after the meat is ready. **(6)** Divide the cooked rice noodles among serving dishes to serve. Over the noodles, ladle the boiling soup and steak. **(7)** Add some bean sprouts, lime wedges, and fresh cilantro leaves as garnish. Enjoy while hot!

PAPRIKA BEEF PHO

Preparation Time: 15 minutes || Cooking Time: 2 hours || Servings: 4

Ingredients:

8 cups beef broth	1 lb beef brisket, thinly sliced
2 tablespoons paprika	1 onion, thinly sliced
3 cloves garlic, minced	1 tablespoon ginger, grated
2 tablespoons fish sauce	1 tablespoon soy sauce
1 tablespoon brown sugar	8 oz rice noodles
Fresh basil leaves, thinly sliced red chili, lime wedges for garnish	

Instructions:

(1) Simmer the beef stock in a large saucepan over medium heat. **(2)** Toss in the sliced beef brisket, brown sugar, soy sauce, onion, garlic, ginger, paprika, and fish sauce. Mix everything together. **(3)** Simmer the stock for one and a half to two hours or until the meat is very soft and the flavors are thoroughly combined. **(4)** While waiting, cook and drain the rice noodles according to the instructions. **(5)** Taste the steak after it's soft and adjust the spices if needed. **(6)** Divide the cooked rice noodles among serving dishes to serve. Over the noodles, ladle the boiling soup and steak. **(7)** Add lime wedges, thinly sliced red Chile, and fresh basil leaves as garnish. Enjoy while hot!

JALAPENO BEEF PHO

Preparation Time: 20 minutes || Cooking Time: 2 hours || Servings: 4

Ingredients:

8 cups beef broth	1 lb beef flank steak, thinly sliced
2 jalapenos, thinly sliced	1 onion, thinly sliced
3 cloves garlic, minced	1 tablespoon ginger, grated
2 tablespoons fish sauce	1 tablespoon soy sauce
1 tablespoon brown sugar	8 oz rice noodles

Fresh mint leaves,
sliced green onion,
lime wedges for
garnish

Instructions:

(1) Simmer the beef stock in a large saucepan over medium heat. **(2)** Toss in the cut beef flank steak, jalapenos, onion, garlic, ginger, brown sugar, fish sauce, and soy sauce. Mix everything together. **(3)** Simmer the stock for one and a half to two hours or until the meat is very soft and the flavors are thoroughly combined. **(4)** While waiting, cook and drain the rice noodles according to the instructions. **(5)** Taste the steak after its soft and adjust the spices if needed. **(6)** Divide the cooked rice noodles among serving dishes to serve. Over the noodles, ladle the boiling soup and steak. **(7)** Add lime wedges, sliced green onions, and fresh mint leaves as garnish. Enjoy while hot!

TRUFFLE BEEF PHO

Preparation Time: 20 minutes || Cooking Time: 2 hours || Servings: 4

Ingredients:

1 pound beef brisket, thinly sliced	8 cups beef broth
2 onions, halved	4 cloves garlic, minced
1-inch piece ginger, sliced	2 cinnamon sticks
4-star anise	4 cloves
1 tablespoon fish sauce	1 tablespoon sugar
Salt and pepper to taste	8 ounces rice noodles
1 cup bean sprouts	1/2 cup sliced green onions
Fresh cilantro leaves for garnish	1 tablespoon truffle oil
Lime wedges for serving	

Instructions:

(1) In a big saucepan, mix beef broth, onions, garlic, ginger, cinnamon sticks, star anise, cloves, fish sauce, sugar, salt, and pepper. Bring to a boil. **(2)** Simmer on low for 1.5 hours to blend flavors. **(3)** Meanwhile, make rice noodles according to package instructions. Drain and set aside. **(4)** After 1.5 hours, remove onions, garlic, ginger, cinnamon sticks, star anise, and cloves from broth. **(5)** Simmer the sliced beef brisket in the stock for 30 minutes until done. **(6)** Divide cooked rice noodles into bowls to serve. Place cooked beef brisket on top. **(7)** Cover noodles and meat with heated broth. **(8)** Add bean sprouts, green onions, cilantro, and truffle oil. **(9)** Heat and serve with lime wedges.

SESAME BEEF PHO

Preparation Time: 25 minutes || Cooking Time: 2 hours || Servings: 4

Ingredients:

1 pound beef sirloin, thinly sliced	8 cups beef broth
2 onions, halved	4 cloves garlic, minced
1-inch piece ginger, sliced	2 cinnamon sticks
4-star anise	4 cloves
1 tablespoon soy sauce	1 tablespoon sesame oil
1 tablespoon sugar	Salt and pepper to taste
8 ounces rice noodles	1 cup sliced mushrooms
1/2 cup sliced green onions	Fresh cilantro leaves for garnish
1 tablespoon toasted sesame seeds	Lime wedges for serving

Instructions:

(1) In a large saucepan, add beef broth, onions, garlic, ginger, cinnamon sticks, star anise, cloves, soy sauce, sesame oil, sugar, salt, and pepper. Bring to a boil. **(2)** Simmer on low for 1.5 hours to blend flavors. **(3)** Meanwhile, make rice noodles according to package instructions. Drain and set aside. **(4)** After 1.5 hours, remove onions, garlic, ginger, cinnamon sticks, star anise, and cloves from broth. **(5)** Add sliced beef sirloin and mushrooms to the stock and simmer for 30 minutes to cook. **(6)** Divide cooked rice noodles into bowls to serve. Put mushrooms and cooked beef sirloin on top. **(7)** Add heated broth to noodles, meat, and mushrooms. **(8)** Add chopped green onions, cilantro, and toasted sesame seeds. **(9)** Heat and serve with lime wedges.

CUMIN BEEF PHO

Preparation Time: 20 minutes || Cooking Time: 2 hours || Servings: 4

Ingredients:

1 pound beef brisket, thinly sliced	8 cups beef broth
2 onions, thinly sliced	4 cloves garlic, minced
2-inch piece ginger, sliced	2 tablespoons cumin seeds
2 cinnamon sticks	4-star anise
1 tablespoon coriander seeds	1 tablespoon fish sauce
1 tablespoon soy sauce	1 tablespoon sugar
Salt and pepper to taste	8 ounces dried rice noodles
Fresh cilantro, Thai basil, bean sprouts, lime wedges for serving	

Instructions:

(1) Toast cumin seeds, cinnamon sticks, star anise, and coriander seeds for 2 minutes in a big saucepan over medium heat until aromatic. **(2)** Set the pot on high heat and add the ginger, fish sauce, soy sauce, sugar, salt, and pepper. Low-heat simmer for 1 hour after boiling. **(3)** Add the sliced beef brisket and simmer for another hour until tender. **(4)** Meanwhile, make rice noodles according to package instructions. **(5)** Taste and season the soup once the meat is tender. **(6)** Divide cooked noodles into bowls to serve. Cover noodles with heated broth and meat. Garnish with cilantro, Thai basil, bean sprouts, and lime juice.

ROSEMARY BEEF PHO

Preparation Time: 30 minutes || Cooking Time: 3 hours || Servings: 4

Ingredients:

1 pound beef shank, thinly sliced	8 cups beef stock
2 onions, sliced	4 cloves garlic, minced
2-inch piece ginger, sliced	2 tablespoons fresh rosemary leaves
2 cinnamon sticks	4 cloves
1 tablespoon fish sauce	1 tablespoon soy sauce
1 tablespoon sugar	Salt and pepper to taste
8 ounces dried rice noodles	Fresh cilantro, mint, bean sprouts, lime wedges for serving

Instructions:

(1) Add the onions, garlic, ginger, cloves, cinnamon sticks, rosemary leaves, fish sauce, soy sauce, sugar, salt, and pepper to a big saucepan. Reduce heat and simmer for two hours after boiling. **(2)** When the meat is cooked, add the sliced beef shank to the stew and simmer for an additional hour. **(3)** Meanwhile, the beef cooks the rice noodles per the box. **(4)** Taste the broth once the meat is soft and adjust the seasoning if needed. **(5)** The cooked noodles should be divided into serving dishes for serving. Over the noodles, ladle the boiling soup and steak. Add some fresh cilantro, mint, bean sprouts, and lime juice as garnish.

CHAPTER: 3 CHICKEN PHO VARIATIONS:

CLASSIC CHICKEN PHO

Preparation Time: 30 minutes || Cooking Time: 2 hours || Servings: 4

Ingredients:

Ingredients:

1 whole chicken, cut into pieces	2 onions, peeled and halved
3-inch piece of ginger, sliced	2 cinnamon sticks
4-star anise	5 cloves
1 tablespoon coriander seeds	1 tablespoon salt
1 tablespoon sugar	8 cups water
8 ounces dried rice noodles	

Garnishes: bean sprouts, Thai basil, cilantro, lime wedges, thinly sliced chili peppers, hoisin sauce, Sriracha sauce

Instructions:

(1) Lightly blacken onions and ginger over an open flame or broiler. **(2)** Roast cinnamon sticks, star anise, cloves, and coriander seeds for 2 minutes in a big saucepan until aromatic. **(3)** Chicken chunks, charred onions, ginger, salt, sugar, and water should be added to the saucepan. **(4)** After boiling, decrease heat to low and simmer for 1.5 to 2 hours, skimming impurities. **(5)** Remove chicken from soup and shred. Set aside. **(6)** Strain broth into a clean saucepan using a fine-mesh screen or cheesecloth. Get rid of solids. **(7)** Follow the package instructions to cook rice noodles. **(8)** Sprinkle shredded chicken over cooked noodles in serving dishes. **(9)** Add heated broth to noodles and chicken. **(10)** Serve toppings on the side so diners may personalize their pho.

SPICY LEMONGRASS CHICKEN PHO

Preparation Time: 45 minutes || Cooking Time: 1 hour || Servings: 4

Ingredients:

1 whole chicken, cut into pieces	2 stalks lemongrass, outer layers removed, thinly sliced
3 Thai bird's eye chili peppers, thinly sliced	2 shallots, thinly sliced
3 cloves garlic, minced	1 tablespoon fish sauce
1 tablespoon sugar	1 tablespoon salt
8 cups chicken broth	8 ounces dried rice noodles

Garnishes: bean sprouts, Thai basil, cilantro, lime wedges, thinly sliced chili peppers, hoisin sauce, Sriracha sauce

Instructions:

(1) Chicken, lemongrass, chili peppers, shallots, garlic, fish sauce, sugar, salt, and chicken broth should all be combined in a big saucepan. **(2)** Once you've brought it to a boil, lower the heat and simmer it for 45 to 1 hour. **(3)** After taking the chicken out of the soup, shred the flesh. Put away. **(4)** Cook rice noodles according to the box. **(5)** To present, distribute the cooked noodles into serving bowls and place shredded chicken on top. **(6)** Over the noodles and chicken, ladle the heated broth. **(7)** Let each diner customize their pho by serving with toppings on the side.

COCONUT CURRY CHICKEN PHO

Preparation Time: 40 minutes || Cooking Time: 1 hour 30 minutes || Servings: 4

Ingredients:

1 whole chicken, cut into pieces	1 can (14 ounces) coconut milk
2 tablespoons red curry paste	2 tablespoons fish sauce
1 tablespoon sugar	1 tablespoon salt
8 cups chicken broth	8 ounces dried rice noodles

Garnishes: bean sprouts, Thai basil, cilantro, lime wedges, thinly sliced chili peppers, hoisin sauce, Sriracha sauce

Instructions:

(1) The chicken, fish sauce, coconut milk, red curry paste, sugar, salt, and chicken broth should all be combined in a big saucepan. **(2)** Reduce heat to a simmer for 1–1.5 hours after boiling. **(3)** Shred the chicken flesh after removing it from the soup. Put aside. **(4)** The packet will tell you how to cook the rice noodles. **(5)** To present, portion up the cooked noodles into serving bowls and garnish with chicken shreds. **(6)** Pour the steaming broth over the chicken and noodles. **(7)** To allow each diner to personalize their pho, serve with garnishes on the side.

GINGER CHICKEN PHO WITH BOK CHOY

Preparation Time: 30 minutes || Cooking Time: 1 hour || Servings: 4

Ingredients:

- 1 lb chicken breast
- 2 inches fresh ginger, thinly sliced
- 1 cinnamon stick
- 2 tablespoons fish sauce
- 2 Bok choy, sliced
- 1/4 cup cilantro, chopped
- Salt and pepper, to taste
- 8 cups chicken broth
- 2-star anise
- 4 cloves
- 200g rice noodles
- 4 green onions, thinly sliced
- Lime wedges for serving

Instructions:

(1) Mix chicken broth, ginger, star anise, cinnamon, and cloves in a big saucepan. After boiling, decrease the heat and simmer for 20 minutes to blend flavors. **(2)** Place the chicken breast in the saucepan and poach for 20 minutes over medium heat until done. Leave the chicken to cool, then shred. **(3)** Return spices to saucepan after straining broth. Season with fish sauce, salt, and pepper. **(4)** Drain rice noodles and set aside after cooking according to package instructions. **(5)** Cookbook choy for 3 minutes in boiling broth. **(6)** Add noodles, shredded chicken, book choy, and heated broth to bowls. Add green onions, cilantro, and lime wedges.

FIVE-SPICE CHICKEN PHO

Preparation Time: 20 minutes || Cooking Time: 1 hour || Servings: 4

Ingredients:

- 1 lb chicken thighs
- 1 onion, halved and charred
- 1 tablespoon five-spice powder
- 200g flat rice noodles
- 1/2 cup basil leaves
- Hoisin sauce for serving
- Salt, to taste
- 8 cups chicken broth
- 1 ginger piece (3 inches), halved and charred
- 2 tablespoons fish sauce
- 1 cup bean sprouts
- 4 lime wedges
- Sriracha sauce for serving

Instructions:

(1) The chicken stock should be brought to a boil in a big saucepan. Stir in the ginger, five-spice powder, and the charred onion. Allow to simmer for half an hour. **(2)** After adding the chicken thighs to the stock, simmer for 20 minutes or until the chicken is tender. Remove and shred the chicken, then set it aside. **(3)** After removing the particles using a strainer, add the broth back to the saucepan. Add salt and fish sauce for seasoning. **(4)** After cooking rice noodles as directed on the package, drain. **(5)** To serve, divide the chicken and noodles among the dishes. Serve with bean sprouts, basil, lime wedges, hoisin sauce, and Sriracha sauce on the side after ladling hot broth over everything.

SRIRACHA CHICKEN PHO

Preparation Time: 15 minutes || Cooking Time: 45 minutes || Servings: 4

Ingredients:

- 1 lb chicken breast
- 1 tablespoon olive oil
- 3 garlic cloves, minced
- 2 tablespoons Sriracha sauce, plus more for serving
- 200g rice noodles
- 2 green onions, sliced
- Lime wedges for serving
- 8 cups chicken broth
- 1 onion, sliced
- 1 tablespoon grated ginger
- 1 tablespoon soy sauce
- 1 cup thinly sliced mushrooms
- Fresh cilantro for garnish

Instructions:

(1) A big saucepan set over medium heat should be used to heat the olive oil. Add onion, garlic, and ginger and sauté for three minutes until fragrant. **(2)** Put soy sauce, Sriracha sauce, and chicken broth in there. Raise to a simmer. **(3)** When the chicken breasts are cooked through, which should take 20 minutes, add them to the soup. Pull out the chicken, shred it, and put it aside. **(4)** See package directions for cooking and draining rice noodles. **(5)** Once the mushrooms are soft, add them to the stock and boil for 5 minutes. **(6)** Spoon noodles into bowls, add shredded chicken on top and then pour hot broth and mushrooms over. Add some cilantro and green onions as a garnish and serve with more Sriracha and lime wedges on the side.

CILANTRO-LIME CHICKEN PHO

Preparation Time: 20 minutes || Cooking Time: 1 hour || Servings: 4

Ingredients:

1 lb chicken breasts	8 cups chicken stock
1 onion, halved and charred	4 garlic cloves, smashed
2-inch piece of ginger, sliced	2 limes, juiced
1 bunch cilantro, chopped	200g rice noodles
2 tablespoons fish sauce	Salt, to taste
Garnishes: lime wedges, sliced jalapeños, bean sprouts, and fresh cilantro leaves	

Instructions:

(1) Boil chicken stock in a large pot. With the chicken breasts, add ginger, garlic, and caramelized onion. Cook for 30 minutes at a simmer once the chicken is done. **(2)** After taking the chicken out of the pot, shred it. After straining, pour the broth back into the pot. **(3)** Mix fish sauce and lime juice into soup. Sprinkle salt on meals before serving. **(4)** As directed on the package, prepare the rice noodles. **(5)** Spoon noodles into each bowl. Add shredded chicken over top and cover with heated broth. **(6)** Add fresh cilantro, bean sprouts, jalapeños, and lime wedges as garnish. Serve right away.

THAI BASIL CHICKEN PHO

Preparation Time: 20 minutes || Cooking Time: 1 hour || Servings: 4

Ingredients:

1 lb chicken thighs, bone-in	8 cups chicken stock
1 onion, halved and charred	4 garlic cloves, smashed
2-inch piece of ginger, sliced	1-star anise
1 cinnamon stick	2 tablespoons soy sauce
1 tablespoon fish sauce	200g rice noodles
1 bunch Thai basil leaves	Garnishes: bean sprouts, sliced red chili, lime wedges, and Thai basil leaves

Instructions:

(1) Chicken stock, charred onion, garlic, ginger, star anise, and cinnamon stick go into a big skillet with the chicken thighs. Boil for 45 minutes, then lower the heat. **(2)** After taking out the chicken, shred it and throw away the bones. After straining, pour the broth back into the pot. **(3)** Mix in fish and soy sauce. Change the flavor as needed. **(4)** Simply follow the steps on the package to make the rice noodles. **(5)** Spoon noodles into bowls, add shredded chicken on top, then cover with heated broth. **(6)** Add bean sprouts, Thai basil, lime wedges, and red Chile as garnish. Serve right away.

ROASTED GARLIC CHICKEN PHO

Preparation Time: 15 minutes (plus 45 minutes for roasting garlic) || Cooking Time: 1 hour || Servings: 4

Ingredients:

1 whole garlic bulb	1 lb chicken breasts
8 cups chicken stock	1 onion, halved and charred
2-inch piece of ginger, sliced	200g rice noodles
2 tablespoons fish sauce	Salt, to taste
Garnishes: sliced green onions, cilantro leaves, lime wedges, and thinly sliced chili	

Instructions:

(1) Set oven temperature to 400°F, or 200°C. Cut off the top of the garlic bulb, cover with foil, pour oil over it, and roast it for forty-five minutes. Squeeze the garlic cloves out when they've cooled. **(2)** The chicken stock should be brought to a boil in a big saucepan. Add the ginger, roasted garlic cloves, charred onion, and chicken breasts. Allow to simmer for half an hour. **(3)** After taking it out, shred the chicken and put it back in the saucepan. After straining the soup, put it back in the pot. **(4)** Add fish sauce and stir. Add salt to taste to season. **(5)** Peel and boil the rice noodles as directed on the package. **(6)** Put noodles, chicken, and hot broth in dishes. Add some Chile, lime wedges, cilantro, and green onions as garnish. Serve right away.

SMOKED PAPRIKA CHICKEN PHO

Preparation Time: 30 minutes || Cooking Time: 1 hour || Servings: 4 servings

Ingredients:

1 lb chicken breast	2 tablespoons smoked paprika
1 tablespoon olive oil	4 cups chicken broth
2 cups water	200g rice noodles
1 onion, thinly sliced	2 cloves garlic, minced
1-inch ginger, grated	2-star anise
1 cinnamon stick	1 tablespoon fish sauce
Salt and pepper, to taste	Fresh cilantro for garnish
Lime wedges for serving	Bean sprouts for serving
Sliced jalapeños for serving	

Instructions:

(1) Toss the chicken breasts with smoked paprika, salt, and pepper. **(2)** Use a large pot to heat olive oil on medium. Season the chicken and sear for 3–4 minutes every side. Hold and remove. **(3)** Add onion, garlic, and ginger to a saucepan. Sauté until fragrant, 2 minutes. **(4)** Add chicken broth and water. Cook with star anise and cinnamon. **(5)** Return the chicken to the saucepan, lower the heat, and simmer for 30 minutes until done. **(6)** After cooling, shred the chicken into bite-sized pieces. **(7)** Place rice noodles in the saucepan and cook per package instructions. **(8)** Put shredded chicken back in the pot. Season with salt and pepper after adding fish sauce. **(9)** Serve pho in bowls with cilantro, lime wedges, bean sprouts, and jalapeño slices.

HONEY SESAME CHICKEN PHO

Preparation Time: 20 minutes || Cooking Time: 45 minutes || Servings: 4 servings

Ingredients:

1 lb chicken breast	2 tablespoons honey
1 tablespoon sesame oil	1 tablespoon soy sauce
4 cups chicken broth	2 cups water
200g rice noodles	1 onion, thinly sliced
2 cloves garlic, minced	1-inch ginger, grated
2-star anise	1 cinnamon stick
1 tablespoon fish sauce	Salt and pepper, to taste
Fresh cilantro for garnish	Lime wedges for serving
Bean sprouts for serving	Sliced green onions for serving
Sesame seeds, for garnish	

Instructions:

(1) Mix honey, sesame oil, and soy sauce in a bowl. Marinate the chicken breast for 15 minutes. **(2)** Heat a big saucepan on medium. Brown the marinated chicken on both sides and cook thoroughly, 5-6 minutes per side. Remove and reserve. **(3)** Add onion, garlic, and ginger to a saucepan. Sauté until fragrant, 2 minutes. **(4)** Add water, star anise, and cinnamon stick to chicken broth. Simmer for 20 minutes after boiling. **(5)** Follow package instructions to cook rice noodles. **(6)** Shred cooked chicken into bite-sized pieces. **(7)** Chicken and noodles should be added to the broth. Season with salt and pepper after adding fish sauce. **(8)** Add cilantro, lime wedges, bean sprouts, sliced green onions, and sesame seeds to bowls of pho.

TERIYAKI CHICKEN PHO

Preparation Time: 25 minutes || Cooking Time: 50 minutes || Servings: 4 servings

Ingredients:

1 lb chicken breast	¼ cup teriyaki sauce
1 tablespoon vegetable oil	4 cups chicken broth
2 cups water	200g rice noodles
1 onion, thinly sliced	2 cloves garlic, minced
1-inch ginger, grated	2-star anise
1 cinnamon stick	1 tablespoon fish sauce
Salt and pepper, to taste	Fresh basil for garnish
Lime wedges for serving	Bean sprouts for serving
Sliced red chili for serving	

Instructions:

(1) Teriyaki-marinate the chicken breast for 30 minutes. **(2)** In a big saucepan, heat vegetable oil on medium. Add marinated chicken and fry for 5-6 minutes per side until browned and cooked through. Take out and set. **(3)** Mix onion, garlic, and ginger in the saucepan. Sauté 2 minutes until fragrant. **(4)** Put chicken broth and water in. Include star anise and cinnamon. Simmer for 25 minutes after boiling. **(5)** Cook rice noodles as directed. **(6)** Shred cooked chicken into small pieces. **(7)** Combine shredded chicken and noodles with broth. Add fish sauce and salt and pepper. **(8)** Add basil, lime wedges, bean sprouts, and red Chile to bowls of pho.

CHIPOTLE CHICKEN PHO

Preparation Time: 20 minutes || Cooking Time: 1 hour || Servings: 4

Ingredients:

2 tablespoons olive oil	1 large onion, thinly sliced
4 cloves garlic, minced	1 tablespoon grated ginger
2 chipotle peppers in adobo sauce, chopped very small	1.5 liters of chicken broth
2-star anise	1 cinnamon stick
500g chicken breast, thinly sliced	200g rice noodles
2 tablespoons fish sauce	Extra black pepper and salt, to taste
Garnishes: fresh cilantro, sliced green onions, lime wedges, bean sprouts	

Instructions:

(1) Moderately heat olive oil in a big saucepan. For 5 minutes, sauté the onion, garlic, and ginger until the onion is tender and transparent. **(2)** Cook for 2 more minutes with chipotle peppers. **(3)** Add chicken broth, star anise, and cinnamon. Simmer for 30 minutes after boiling to infuse flavors. **(4)** Simmer chicken breast for 20 minutes in the pot. Shred and set aside the chicken. **(5)** Drain rice noodles after cooking them in a separate pot according to the package instructions. **(6)** Add fish sauce to the soup after removing the star anise and cinnamon stick. Sprinkle salt and pepper. **(7)** Distribute noodles among bowls. Pour heated broth over shredded chicken. Serve with cilantro, green onions, lime wedges, and bean sprouts.

SZECHUAN PEPPER CHICKEN PHO

Preparation Time: 20 minutes || Cooking Time: 1 hour || Servings: 4

Ingredients:

2 tablespoons sesame oil	1 large onion, thinly sliced
4 cloves garlic, minced	1 tablespoon grated ginger
1 tablespoon Szechuan peppercorns, crushed	1.5 liters of chicken broth
2-star anise	1 cinnamon stick
500g chicken breast, thinly sliced	200g rice noodles
2 tablespoons soy sauce	Salt, to taste
Garnishes: fresh cilantro, sliced green onions, lime wedges, bean sprouts, chili oil	

Instructions:

(1) In a big saucepan, heat sesame oil on medium. Cook the onion, garlic, ginger, and Szechuan peppercorns for 5 minutes until tender. **(2)** Add chicken broth, star anise, and cinnamon stick. After boiling, simmer for 30 minutes. **(3)** Cook chicken breast for 20 minutes. Shred and reserve the chicken. **(4)** Cook and drain rice noodles in a separate saucepan per the package instructions. **(5)** Add soy sauce to the soup after removing the star anise and cinnamon stick. Season with salt. **(6)** Serve noodles, shredded chicken, and heated broth in bowls. Top with cilantro, green onions, lime wedges, bean sprouts, and chili oil.

SATAY CHICKEN PHO

Preparation Time: 30 minutes (includes marinating time) || Cooking Time: 1 hour || Servings: 4

Ingredients:

For the Chicken Marinade:

500g chicken breast, thinly sliced	2 tablespoons soy sauce
2 tablespoons peanut butter	1 tablespoon honey
1 clove garlic, minced	1 teaspoon grated ginger

For the Pho:

2 tablespoons vegetable oil	1 large onion, thinly sliced
4 cloves garlic, minced	1 tablespoon grated ginger
1.5 liters of chicken broth	2-star anise
1 cinnamon stick	200g rice noodles
Salt, to taste	Garnishes: fresh cilantro, sliced green onions, lime wedges, bean sprouts, crushed peanuts

Instructions:

(1) Mix chicken marinade ingredients in a basin. Marinate chicken slices for 20 minutes. **(2)** Heat vegetable oil in a big saucepan on medium. Add onion, garlic, and ginger and simmer for 5 minutes to soften the onion. **(3)** Cook marinated chicken till browned and done. **(4)** Add star anise, cinnamon stick, and chicken broth. Lower heat and simmer for 30 minutes after boiling. **(5)** Drain the rice noodles after cooking them per the packet. **(6)** Remove star anise and cinnamon stick from broth. Add salt to taste. **(7)** Serve noodles in dishes with satay chicken and hot broth. Add cilantro, green onions, lime wedges, bean sprouts, and crushed peanuts.

MANGO CHICKEN PHO

Preparation Time: 20 minutes || Cooking Time: 60 minutes || Servings: 4

Ingredients:

2 liters of chicken stock	2 chicken breasts, thinly sliced
200g rice noodles	1 ripe mango, peeled and thinly sliced
1 onion, thinly sliced	3 cloves garlic, minced
1 tablespoon ginger, grated	2-star anise
1 cinnamon stick	2 tablespoons fish sauce
1 tablespoon sugar	Fresh herbs (cilantro, mint)

Bean sprouts, lime wedges, and sliced chili for serving

Instructions:

(1) Boil chicken stock in a big saucepan. Include star anise, cinnamon, garlic, ginger, and onion. Reduce heat and simmer 30 minutes to flavor the broth. **(2)** Return the broth to the pot after straining the solids. Adjust fish sauce and sugar to taste. **(3)** Add chicken pieces to broth over medium heat. Cook chicken for 10-15 minutes until done. **(4)** Prepare rice noodles according to package instructions. **(5)** Divide cooked noodles into dishes to serve. Put mango and chicken pieces on top. Pour hot broth on top. **(6)** Add fresh herbs, bean sprouts, lime wedges, and Chile slices. Serve now.

PINEAPPLE CHICKEN PHO

Preparation Time: 20 minutes || Cooking Time: 60 minutes || Servings: 4

Ingredients:

2 liters of chicken stock	2 chicken breasts, thinly sliced
200g rice noodles	1 cup fresh pineapple, cut into thin slices
1 onion, thinly sliced	3 cloves garlic, minced
1 tablespoon ginger, grated	2-star anise
1 cinnamon stick	2 tablespoons fish sauce
1 tablespoon sugar	Fresh herbs (cilantro, basil)
Bean sprouts, lime wedges, and sliced chili for serving	

Instructions:

(1) The chicken stock should be brought to a boil in a big saucepan. Add the onion, ginger, garlic, star anise, and cinnamon stick. Simmer for 30 minutes on low heat. **(2)** After straining, pour the broth back into the pot. Add sugar and fish sauce, tasting as you go. **(3)** Add the chicken chunks to the medium-heated stock and simmer for 10–15 minutes until done. **(4)** Do what the package says to make the rice noodles. **(5)** Place noodles in bowls, top with chicken and pineapple, then cover with hot broth to assemble the pho. **(6)** Add some Chile, lime wedges, bean sprouts, and herbs as garnish. Warm up the food.

CASHEW CHICKEN PHO

Preparation Time: 20 minutes || Cooking Time: 60 minutes || Servings: 4

Ingredients:

2 liters of chicken stock	2 chicken breasts, thinly sliced
200g rice noodles	½ cup roasted cashews, roughly chopped
1 onion, thinly sliced	3 cloves garlic, minced
1 tablespoon ginger, grated	2-star anise
1 cinnamon stick	2 tablespoons fish sauce
1 tablespoon sugar	Fresh herbs (cilantro, basil)
Bean sprouts, lime wedges, and sliced chili for serving	

Instructions:

(1) In a big saucepan, bring the chicken stock to a boil. Add the onion, ginger, garlic, cinnamon, and star anise. Allow to simmer for half an hour. **(2)** After straining, put the soup back into the saucepan and add sugar and fish sauce to taste. **(3)** When the soup is simmering, add the chicken and cook it through. **(4)** Peel and boil the rice noodles as directed on the package. **(5)** To serve, arrange noodles in bowls, add chicken on top, and then garnish with cashews. Pour heated broth over the top. **(6)** Add some herbs, bean sprouts, lime, and chili as garnish. Savor it hot.

PEANUT CHICKEN PHO

Preparation Time: 20 minutes || Cooking Time: 30 minutes || Servings: 4

Ingredients:

1 liter chicken broth	2 chicken breasts, thinly sliced
200g rice noodles	1 tablespoon olive oil
3 cloves garlic, minced	1 tablespoon ginger, grated
2 tablespoons soy sauce	1 tablespoon fish sauce
2 tablespoons peanut butter	1 teaspoon sugar
Salt and pepper, to taste	2 spring onions, chopped
1 handful fresh cilantro, chopped	1 lime, cut into wedges
1 red chili, sliced (optional)	1 handful bean sprouts (optional)
Crushed peanuts for garnish	

Instructions:

(1) Put the olive oil in a big pot and set it over medium heat. Ginger and garlic should be aromatic after two minutes. **(2)** Add the sugar, peanut butter, fish sauce, soy sauce, and chicken stock and stir. Heat through to a simmer. **(3)** After adding the chicken pieces to the stock, simmer them for ten to fifteen minutes or until they are no longer pink. **(4)** As you wait, make the rice noodles as directed on the package. **(5)** While the broth is being prepared, season it to taste with salt and pepper. **(6)** Spoon cooked noodles into dishes to serve. Over the noodles, ladle the heated broth and chicken chunks. **(7)** Add bean sprouts, crushed peanuts, lime wedges, cilantro, and spring onions as garnish. Serve right away.

LEMONGRASS-COCONUT CHICKEN PHO

Preparation Time: 15 minutes || Cooking Time: 25 minutes || Servings: 4

Ingredients:

1 liter chicken broth	1 can (400ml) coconut milk
2 chicken breasts, thinly sliced	200g rice noodles
2 stalks lemongrass, bruised and chopped	1 tablespoon olive oil
3 cloves garlic, minced	1 tablespoon ginger, grated
2 tablespoons fish sauce	1 teaspoon sugar
Salt and pepper, to taste	2 spring onions, chopped
1 handful fresh cilantro, chopped	1 lime, cut into wedges
1 red chili, sliced (optional)	1 handful bean sprouts (optional)

Instructions:

(1) Warm up the olive oil in a big saucepan over medium heat. Add the ginger, garlic, and lemongrass, and sauté for two to three minutes or until fragrant. **(2)** Add the coconut milk and chicken broth. Heat through to a simmer. **(3)** Add the sugar and fish sauce, and then stir in the chicken chunks. Cook for ten to fifteen minutes or until the chicken is well done. **(4)** As directed on the package, prepare the rice noodles. **(5)** While the broth is being prepared, season it to taste with salt and pepper. **(6)** Spoon cooked noodles into dishes to serve. Over the noodles, pour the heated broth and the chicken pieces. **(7)** Add bean sprouts, lime wedges, cilantro, red Chile, and spring onions as garnish. Serve right away.

GREEN CURRY CHICKEN PHO

Preparation Time: 20 minutes || Cooking Time: 30 minutes || Servings: 4

Ingredients:

1 liter chicken broth	2 chicken breasts, thinly sliced
200g rice noodles	1 tablespoon olive oil
3 cloves garlic, minced	1 tablespoon ginger, grated
3 tablespoons green	1 can (400ml) coconut

curry paste
1 tablespoon fish sauce
Salt and pepper, to taste
1 handful fresh cilantro, chopped
1 red chili, sliced (optional)

milk
1 teaspoon sugar
2 spring onions, chopped
1 lime, cut into wedges
1 handful bean sprouts (optional)

Instructions:

(1) Warm up the olive oil in a big saucepan over medium heat. Cook the green curry paste, garlic, and ginger for two minutes or until aromatic. **(2)** After adding the coconut milk and chicken broth, stir and heat through. **(3)** Add the sugar and fish sauce, followed by the chicken pieces. Simmer the chicken for ten to fifteen minutes or until it is no longer pink. **(4)** As you wait, make the rice noodles as directed on the package. **(5)** While the broth is being prepared, season it to taste with salt and pepper. **(6)** Divide the cooked noodles among dishes for serving. Over the noodles, ladle the heated broth and chicken chunks. **(7)** Add bean sprouts, lime wedges, cilantro, red Chile, and spring onions as garnish. Serve right away.

RED CURRY CHICKEN PHO

Preparation Time: 20 minutes || Cooking Time: 1 hour || Servings: 4

Ingredients:

1 tablespoon oil	2 tablespoons red curry paste
6 cups chicken broth	1 can (14 ounces) coconut milk
1-pound boneless, skinless chicken breast, thinly sliced	200 grams of rice noodles
1 tablespoon fish sauce, or to taste	1 tablespoon sugar
Salt, to taste	Garnishes: bean sprouts, lime wedges, sliced red onion, fresh cilantro, and sliced chilies

Instructions:

(1) In a big saucepan, warm the oil over medium heat. Fry the red curry paste for one to two minutes or until it becomes aromatic. **(2)** Mix coconut milk with chicken broth. Lower the heat and simmer for five minutes after boiling. **(3)** After adding the chicken pieces to the saucepan, simmer for 15 to 20 minutes or until the chicken is well cooked. **(4)** While chicken cooks, prepare rice noodles following package directions. Set aside after draining. **(5)** While the soup is cooking, season with salt, sugar, and fish sauce. **(6)** Divide the noodles into four dishes for serving. Over the noodles, ladle the hot soup and chicken. Present the garnishes separately so that guests may customize them to their taste.

TOM YUM CHICKEN PHO

Preparation Time: 15 minutes || Cooking Time: 45 minutes || Servings: 4

Ingredients:

1 tablespoon oil	2 tablespoons tom yum paste
6 cups chicken broth	1 stalk lemongrass, bruised
3 kaffir lime leaves	1-pound boneless, skinless chicken breast, cut very thinly
200 grams of rice noodles	1 tablespoon fish sauce, or to taste
1 tablespoon lime juice	Salt, to taste
Garnishes: bean sprouts, lime wedges, sliced mushrooms, fresh cilantro, and sliced chilies	

Instructions:

(1) Medium-heat oil in a large pot. Kaffir lime leaves, lemongrass, and tom yum paste. For 2–3 minutes, fry until fragrant. **(2)** Make chicken broth boil. For flavor, decrease the heat and simmer the soup for 20 minutes. **(3)** After adding the chicken pieces, simmer for 15 to 20 minutes or until done. **(4)** After preparing the rice noodles according to the directions on the package, drain them and put them aside. **(5)** Remove lime leaves and lemongrass from the soup. Season soup with fish sauce, lime juice, and salt to taste. **(6)** To serve, arrange noodles in dishes, pour soup and chicken over them, then top with any garnishes.

LEMONGRASS-GINGER CHICKEN PHO

Preparation Time: 20 minutes || Cooking Time: 1 hour || Servings: 4

Ingredients:

1 tablespoon oil	2 stalks lemongrass, finely chopped
2-inch piece of ginger peeled and sliced	6 cups chicken broth
1 pound boneless, skinless chicken breast, cut very thinly	200 grams of rice noodles
1 tablespoon fish sauce, or to taste	1 tablespoon sugar
Salt, to taste	Garnishes: bean sprouts, lime wedges, fresh mint, fresh basil, and sliced chilies

Instructions:

(1) In a big saucepan, warm the oil over medium heat. Sauté the ginger and lemongrass for two to three minutes or until aromatic. **(2)** When it comes to a boil, add the chicken broth. For thirty minutes, simmer over low heat to let the flavors mingle. **(3)** After the chicken is no longer pink, return it to the pot and cook for 15–20 minutes. **(4)** Drain and set aside the rice noodles after cooking them according to the instructions. **(5)** While the soup is cooking, season with salt, sugar, and fish sauce. **(6)** To serve, arrange noodles in bowls, cover with soup and chicken, and provide toppings for personalization on the side.

LEMONGRASS-CHILI CHICKEN PHO

Preparation Time: 15 minutes || Cooking Time: 1 hour || Servings: 4

Ingredients:

8 cups chicken broth	2 lemongrass stalks, trimmed and bruised
2 boneless, skinless chicken breasts	1 tablespoon fish sauce
2 cloves garlic, minced	1 tablespoon grated ginger
2 red chilies, sliced	200g rice noodles
1 cup bean sprouts	Fresh cilantro leaves for garnish
Lime wedges for serving	

Instructions:

(1) Heat the chicken stock in a big saucepan until it boils. Add the fish sauce, garlic, ginger, chili, and lemongrass. Let it simmer for half an hour. **(2)** After cooking, add chicken breasts to stock and boil for 20–25 minutes. Put the chicken aside after shredding. **(3)** As directed on the package, prepare the rice noodles. **(4)** Divide the noodles into dishes, then add the bean sprouts, cilantro, and shredded chicken on top. Overtop, ladle heated broth. Present with lime wedges.

LEMONGRASS-COCONUT CURRY CHICKEN PHO

Preparation Time: 20 minutes || Cooking Time: 45 minutes || Servings: 4

Ingredients:

6 cups chicken broth	2 lemongrass stalks, chopped
1 can (14 oz) coconut milk	2 tablespoons red curry paste
2 boneless, skinless chicken thighs	1 tablespoon fish sauce
1 tablespoon brown sugar	200g rice noodles
1 cup sliced mushrooms	1 red bell pepper, thinly sliced
Fresh basil leaves for garnish	

Instructions:

(1) Mix coconut milk, red curry paste, lemongrass, and chicken broth in a large pot.

Cook till simmering. **(2)** Stir in brown sugar, fish sauce, and chicken thighs. Simmer until the chicken is well cooked, about 30 minutes. **(3)** Follow the product instructions to cook rice noodles. **(4)** Cook the bell pepper and sliced mushrooms in the saucepan for an additional five to seven minutes. **(5)** To serve, divide the noodles among dishes and add the bell pepper, mushrooms, and sliced chicken on top. Spoon hot stock over the surface. Add some fresh basil leaves as garnish.

LEMONGRASS-CILANTRO CHICKEN PHO

Preparation Time: 15 minutes || Cooking Time: 40 minutes || Servings: 4

Ingredients:

8 cups chicken broth	2 lemongrass stalks, thinly sliced
2 boneless, skinless chicken thighs	1 tablespoon soy sauce
1 tablespoon rice vinegar	2 cloves garlic, minced
1 tablespoon grated ginger	200g rice noodles
1 cup shredded cabbage	Fresh cilantro leaves for garnish

Instructions:

(1) Boil chicken stock in a large pot. Stir in ginger, garlic, rice vinegar, lemongrass, and soy sauce. Simmer for 30 minutes. **(2)** Cook the chicken thighs in the stock for 20 to 25 minutes or until they are well-cooked. Take out the chicken, shred it, and put it aside. **(3)** Follow the product instructions to cook rice noodles. **(4)** To serve, divide the noodles among dishes and garnish with cilantro, shredded cabbage, and shredded chicken. Spoon hot stock over the surface. Serve right away.

LEMONGRASS-MINT CHICKEN PHO

Preparation Time: 30 minutes || Cooking Time: 1 hour || Servings: 4

Ingredients:

1 large onion, halved and unpeeled	2-inch piece of ginger, halved lengthwise
2 lemongrass stalks, tough outer layers removed, lightly smashed	6 cups chicken broth
2 chicken breasts	Salt, to taste
200g rice noodles	1 cup mint leaves, roughly torn
2 limes, cut into wedges	2-3 tablespoons fish sauce
Bean sprouts, fresh mint leaves, and sliced chili, to garnish	

Instructions:

(1) Turn on the broiler. Broil the onion and ginger for 5 minutes each side on a baking sheet until slightly browned. **(2)** Simmer chicken stock in a big saucepan. Add chicken breasts, ginger, lemongrass, and roasted onion. Sprinkle salt. **(3)** Simmer chicken for 30 minutes on low. After chilling, shred the chicken into bite-sized pieces. **(4)** Return the broth to the pot after straining. Simmer and season with fish sauce. **(5)** Drain rice noodles after cooking according to package directions. **(6)** Divide noodles into bowls. Put shredded chicken, mint leaves, and heated broth on top. **(7)** Add lime wedges, bean sprouts, mint leaves, and sliced chiles for garnish.

LEMONGRASS-GALANGAL CHICKEN PHO

Preparation Time: 30 minutes || Cooking Time: 1 hour || Servings: 4

Ingredients:

1 large onion, quartered	4-inch piece of ginger, halved lengthwise
2 stalks lemongrass, tough outer layers removed, lightly bruised	2-inch piece galangal, sliced
2 lbs chicken bones or wings	8 cups water
2-star anise	1 cinnamon stick

4 cloves
Salt, to taste
400g rice noodles, prepared according to package instructions
2 tbsp fish sauce
1 lb chicken breast, thinly sliced
Garnishes: Lime wedges, fresh cilantro, sliced green onions, mung bean sprouts, sliced chili

Instructions:

(1) On a grill or over an open flame, gently blacken the onion and ginger. To get rid of any soot, rinse under water. **(2)** Add water, charred onion, ginger, lemongrass, galangal, star anise, cinnamon, cloves, and chicken bones to a big saucepan. After bringing to a boil, turn down the heat. Allow to simmer for forty-five minutes. **(3)** Empty the broth by straining out the sediments. Add salt and fish sauce to the soup and return it to the stove. **(4)** After adding the chicken breast to the stock, boil it for ten to fifteen minutes or until it is done. Take out the chicken, let it cool a little, then shred it. **(5)** Spoon the cooked noodles into individual bowls. Add shredded chicken on top. Cover the noodles and chicken with heated broth. **(6)** Let each person personalize their bowl by serving with toppings on the side.

LEMONGRASS-THAI CHILI CHICKEN PHO

Preparation Time: 30 minutes || Cooking Time: 1 hour || Servings: 4

Ingredients:

1 large onion, quartered
2 stalks lemongrass, tough outer layers removed, lightly bruised
2 lbs. chicken bones or wings
2-star anise
1 tbsp coriander seeds
Salt, to taste
400g rice noodles, prepared according to package instructions
4-inch piece of ginger, halved lengthwise
5 Thai chilis, sliced (adjust to taste)

8 cups water
1 cinnamon stick
2 tbsp fish sauce
1 lb chicken breast, thinly sliced
Garnishes: Lime wedges, fresh cilantro, sliced onions, mung bean sprouts, basil leaves

Instructions:

(1) On a grill or over an open flame, gently blacken the onion and ginger. Use a water rinse to get rid of soot. **(2)** Add water, charred onion, ginger, lemongrass, Thai chilies, star anise, cinnamon, coriander seeds, and chicken bones to a big saucepan. After bringing to a boil, simmer for forty-five minutes on low heat. **(3)** Empty the broth by straining out the sediments. Use salt and fish sauce to season the soup. **(4)** Cook the chicken breast in the stock for ten to fifteen minutes or until it is cooked. Peel, allow to cool, then shred. **(5)** Put the noodles, shredded chicken, and heated broth into the bowls. **(6)** For added flair, serve the dish beside a tray of garnishes.

LEMONGRASS-SOY CHICKEN PHO

Preparation Time: 30 minutes || Cooking Time: 1 hour || Servings: 4

Ingredients:

1 large onion, quartered
2 stalks lemongrass, tough outer layers removed, lightly bruised
8 cups water
1 cinnamon stick
1 tbsp fish sauce
1 lb chicken breast, thinly sliced

Garnishes: Lime wedges, fresh cilantro, sliced green onions, mung bean sprouts
4-inch piece of ginger, halved lengthwise
2 lbs chicken bones or wings

2-star anise
3 tbsp soy sauce
Salt, to taste
400g rice noodles, prepared according to package instructions

Instructions:

(1) Ginger and onion should be lightly browned. To clean rinse. **(2)** In a saucepan, combine water, ginger, lemongrass, charred onion, and chicken bones. Stir in cinnamon and star anise. Boil for 45 minutes, then simmer. **(3)** Strain broth and add to saucepan. Stir in fish and soy sauce. Season with salt. **(4)** Cook the chicken breast in the liquid until it becomes soft. Shred, chill, and remove. **(5)** Put noodles and shredded chicken in dishes. Spoon hot stock over the surface. **(6)** Garnish with parsley for extra taste and texture.

LEMONGRASS-GALANGAL CHICKEN PHO

Preparation Time: 30 minutes || Cooking Time: 1 hour || Servings: 4 servings

Ingredients:

1 lb chicken breasts	8 cups chicken stock
1 stalk lemongrass, bruised and chopped	2-inch piece galangal, sliced
2-star anise	1 cinnamon stick
4 cloves	1 large onion, halved and charred
4 cloves garlic, crushed	2 tablespoons fish sauce
Salt, to taste	200g rice noodles
Garnishes: lime wedges, bean sprouts, sliced green onions, cilantro leaves, sliced chilies	

Instructions:

(1) The chicken stock should be brought to a boil in a big saucepan. Add the cloves, charred onion, garlic, star anise, galangal, lemongrass, and cloves to the chicken breasts. After the chicken is thoroughly cooked, reduce the heat and boil it for around half an hour. **(2)** After taking the chicken out of the saucepan, allow it to cool. Cut the chicken into small shreds. **(3)** After straining, pour the broth back into the pot. To taste, add salt and fish sauce. Maintain the broth's heat on low. **(4)** As directed on the package, prepare the rice noodles. **(5)** Divide the noodles into four dishes for serving. Add shredded chicken on top. Fill each dish with the heated broth. **(6)** As garnish, serve with wedges of lime, bean sprouts, sliced green onions, cilantro, and sliced chilies.

LEMONGRASS-SESAME CHICKEN PHO

Preparation Time: 20 minutes || Cooking Time: 1 hour || Servings: 4

Ingredients:

4 boneless, skinless chicken breasts	8 cups chicken broth
2 stalks lemongrass, sliced	3 cloves garlic, minced
1 onion, thinly sliced	1 tablespoon sesame oil
2 tablespoons soy sauce	1 tablespoon fish sauce
1 tablespoon sesame seeds	8 oz rice noodles
Fresh cilantro leaves, bean sprouts, lime wedges for garnish	

Instructions:

(1) Sesame oil should be heated over medium heat in a big saucepan. Add the onion, lemongrass, and garlic. Cook until aromatic. **(2)** To the saucepan, add fish sauce, soy sauce, and chicken stock. Heat through to a simmer. **(3)** Add cooked chicken breasts to stew and boil for 20–25 minutes. **(4)** After taking the chicken out of the pot, shred it with two forks. Put aside. **(5)** As you wait, prepare the rice noodles per the directions on the box. **(6)** After the noodles are cooked, distribute them among bowls for serving. Add shredded chicken on top. **(7)** Over the chicken and noodles, ladle heated broth. **(8)** Add lime wedges, bean sprouts, cilantro, and sesame seeds as garnish. Warm up the food.

LEMONGRASS-TAMARIND CHICKEN PHO

Preparation Time: 25 minutes || Cooking Time: 45 minutes || Servings: 4

Ingredients:

4 boneless, skinless chicken thighs	8 cups chicken broth
2 stalks lemongrass,	3 cloves garlic, minced

chopped
1 onion, sliced
2 tablespoons fish sauce
Salt and pepper to taste
Fresh Thai basil, mint leaves, sliced chili for garnish

2 tablespoons tamarind paste
1 tablespoon sugar
8 oz rice noodles

Instructions:

(1) Heat some oil in a big saucepan over medium heat. Add the onion, lemongrass, and garlic. Cook until aromatic. **(2)** To the saucepan, add fish sauce, sugar, salt, pepper, and tamarind paste along with the chicken stock. Heat through to a simmer. **(3)** After cooking the chicken, add the thighs to the pot and simmer for 30–35 minutes. **(4)** Take out and shred the chicken from the saucepan, then put it aside. **(5)** How to cook the rice noodles: Read the package and do what it says. **(6)** After the noodles are cooked, distribute them among bowls for serving. Add shredded chicken on top. **(7)** Over the chicken and noodles, ladle heated broth. **(8)** Add sliced chiles, mint leaves, and Thai basil as garnish. Warm up the food.

LEMONGRASS-VINEGAR CHICKEN PHO

Preparation Time: 20 minutes || Cooking Time: 1 hour || Servings: 4

Ingredients:

4 boneless, skinless chicken thighs
2 stalks lemongrass, finely chopped
1 onion, thinly sliced
2 tablespoons fish sauce
Salt and pepper to taste
Fresh cilantro, sliced green onions, sliced jalapenos for garnish

8 cups chicken broth
3 cloves garlic, minced
2 tablespoons rice vinegar
1 tablespoon sugar
8 oz rice noodles

Instructions:

(1) In a big saucepan, warm up some oil over medium heat. Add the onion, lemongrass, and garlic. Cook until aromatic. **(2)** Fill the kettle with chicken broth. Add the sugar, salt, pepper, fish sauce, and rice vinegar. Heat through to a simmer. **(3)** When the chicken is cooked through, add the chicken thighs to the saucepan and simmer for 30 to 35 minutes. **(4)** Take out and shred the chicken from the saucepan, then put it aside. **(5)** How to cook the rice noodles: Read the package and do what it says. **(6)** Spoon cooked noodles into each of the serving dishes. Add shredded chicken on top. **(7)** Over the chicken and noodles, ladle heated broth. **(8)** Add sliced jalapenos, green onions, and cilantro as garnish. Warm up the food.

LEMONGRASS-CORNSTARCH CHICKEN PHO

Preparation Time: 25 minutes || Cooking Time: 50 minutes || Servings: 4

Ingredients:

4 boneless, skinless chicken breasts
2 stalks lemongrass, chopped
1 onion, thinly sliced
2 tablespoons fish sauce
Salt and pepper to taste
Fresh cilantro, sliced scallions, sliced red chilies for garnish

8 cups chicken broth
3 cloves garlic, minced
2 tablespoons cornstarch
1 tablespoon sugar
8 oz rice noodles

Instructions:

(1) In a big saucepan, warm the oil over medium heat. Add the onion, lemongrass, and garlic. Cook until aromatic. **(2)** Fill the kettle with chicken broth. Add the sugar, salt, pepper, and fish sauce. Heat through to a simmer. **(3)** Make a slurry out of cornstarch and a tiny amount of water in a small bowl. **(4)** Stir the cornstarch slurry into the broth until it thickens slightly, stirring constantly. **(5)** Add cooked chicken breasts to stew and boil for 20–25 minutes. **(6)** Take out and shred the chicken from the saucepan, then put it aside. **(7)** How to cook the rice noodles: Read the package and do what it says. **(8)** Spoon cooked noodles into each of the serving dishes. Add shredded chicken on top. **(9)** Over the chicken and noodles, ladle heated broth. **(10)** Add chopped red chiles, scallions, and cilantro as garnish. Warm up the food.

CHAPTER: 4 VEGETARIAN AND VEGAN PHO:

TOFU PHO

Preparation Time: 30 minutes || Cooking Time: 45 minutes || Servings: 4

Ingredients:

4 cups vegetable broth	2 cups water
1 onion, sliced	4 cloves garlic, minced
1-inch piece of ginger, sliced	2-star anise
2 cinnamon sticks	4 cloves
2 tablespoons soy sauce	200g rice noodles
300g firm tofu, pressed and cut into cubes	2 cups bean sprouts
1 cup thinly sliced mushrooms	Fresh herbs (cilantro, basil, mint)
2 limes, cut into wedges	Hoisin sauce and Sriracha (for serving)

Instructions:

(1) The vegetable broth, water, cloves, star anise, onion, garlic, and ginger should all be combined in a big saucepan. **(2)** To blend flavors, decrease the heat and simmer for 30 minutes after boiling. **(3)** After straining, pour the broth back into the pot. Throw away the solids. After adding the soy sauce, taste and adjust the seasoning. **(4)** As directed on the package, prepare the rice noodles; drain and set aside. **(5)** The tofu cubes should be sautéed in a different pan until golden brown all throughout. **(6)** Divide the noodles into four bowls and assemble. Add sliced mushrooms, bean sprouts, and cubes of tofu on top. **(7)** Cover the noodles and toppings with the heated broth. As garnish, serve with lime wedges, fresh herbs, hoisin sauce, and Sriracha on the side.

MUSHROOM PHO

Preparation Time: 25 minutes || Cooking Time: 40 minutes || Servings: 4

Ingredients:

4 cups vegetable broth	2 cups water
1 onion, sliced	4 cloves garlic, minced
1-inch piece of ginger, sliced	1 cinnamon stick
3-star anise	1 teaspoon coriander seeds
2 tablespoons soy sauce	200g rice noodles
3 cups mixed mushrooms (shiitake, oyster, cremini), sliced	2 cups bok choy, chopped
Fresh herbs (cilantro, green onions, basil)	2 limes, cut into wedges
Hoisin sauce and Sriracha (for serving)	

Instructions:

(1) Add water, vegetable broth, ginger, garlic, onion, cinnamon, star anise, and coriander seeds to a big saucepan. After reaching a boil, lower the heat and simmer for 30 minutes. **(2)** After straining, pour the broth back into the pot. Throw away the solids. Add the soy sauce and stir. **(3)** As directed on the package, prepare the rice noodles; drain and set aside. **(4)** To the broth, add the book choy and mushrooms. Simmer the veggies for ten minutes or until they are soft. **(5)** To serve, put the noodles in bowls, top with the veggies and broth, and then top with lime wedges and fresh herbs. Accompany with Sriracha and Hoisin sauce.

VEGETABLE PHO

Preparation Time: 20 minutes || Cooking Time: 30 minutes || Servings: 4

Ingredients:

4 cups vegetable broth	2 cups water
1 onion, sliced	3 cloves garlic, minced
1-inch piece of ginger, sliced	1-star anise
1 cinnamon stick	2 tablespoons soy sauce
200g rice noodles	1 carrot, thinly sliced
1 bell pepper, thinly sliced	1 cup snap peas
1 cup bean sprouts	Fresh herbs (basil, mint, cilantro)
2 limes, cut into wedges	Hoisin sauce and Sriracha (for serving)

Instructions:

(1) Vegetable broth, water, star anise, onion, garlic, and ginger should all be combined in a big saucepan. Start by boiling it, then turn down the heat and let it cook for 20 minutes. **(2)** After straining, pour the broth back into the pot. Throw away the solids. Add the soy sauce and stir. **(3)** As directed on the package, prepare the rice noodles; drain and set aside. **(4)** To the broth, add the bell pepper, carrot, and snap peas. Simmer the veggies for approximately five minutes or until they are crisp but still soft. **(5)** Place noodles in bowls, fill with broth and vegetables, then top with lime wedges, fresh herbs, and bean sprouts. Sriracha and hoisin sauce on the side.

JACKFRUIT PHO

Preparation Time: 30 minutes || Cooking Time: 1 hour || Servings: 4

Ingredients:

2 cans of young green jackfruit, drained and rinsed	8 cups vegetable broth
1 large onion, halved and charred	4 cloves garlic, smashed
1 4-inch piece of ginger, sliced and charred	2 cinnamon sticks
4-star anise	3 cloves
2 tablespoons soy sauce	200g rice noodles
Toppings: bean sprouts, basil leaves, lime wedges, sliced chili, hoisin sauce, and Sriracha	

Instructions:

(1) Using a fork, shred the jackfruit pieces so that they resemble meat and set them aside. **(2)** Vegetable broth, charred onion, garlic, ginger, cinnamon sticks, star anise, and cloves should all be combined in a big saucepan. **(3)** To absorb flavors, decrease the heat and simmer the broth for 30 minutes after boiling. **(4)** After straining the soup and removing the solids, pour the stock back into the saucepan. Add the shredded jackfruit and soy sauce. Simmer for twenty minutes more. **(5)** Drain and set aside rice noodles according to the box directions while the broth simmers. **(6)** Divide the noodles among dishes for serving. Over the noodles, ladle the hot jackfruit broth mixture. Bean sprouts, basil leaves, lime wedges, sliced Chile, hoisin sauce, and Sriracha should be served separately for garnish.

SEITAN PHO

Preparation Time: 15 minutes || Cooking Time: 45 minutes || Servings: 4

Ingredients:

200g seitan, thinly sliced	8 cups vegetable broth
1 large onion, halved and charred	4 cloves garlic, smashed
1 4-inch piece of ginger, sliced and charred	2 cinnamon sticks
4-star anise	3 cloves
2 tablespoons soy sauce	200g rice noodles

Toppings: bean sprouts, basil leaves, lime wedges, sliced chili, hoisin sauce, and Sriracha

Instructions:

(1) Vegetable broth, charred onion, garlic, ginger, cinnamon sticks, star anise, and cloves should all be combined in a big saucepan. After reaching a boil, lower the heat and simmer for 30 minutes. **(2)** After straining the soup and removing the solids, pour the stock back into the saucepan. Add the seitan slices and soy sauce. Allow to simmer for fifteen minutes. **(3)** Drain and set aside rice noodles after following package instructions. **(4)** Divide the noodles among dishes for serving. Over the noodles, ladle the heated seitan broth mixture. Garnish with the suggested toppings and serve.

EGGPLANT PHO

Preparation Time: 20 minutes || Cooking Time: 50 minutes || Servings: 4

Ingredients:

2 medium eggplants, sliced into half-inch thick pieces	8 cups vegetable broth
1 large onion, halved and charred	4 cloves garlic, smashed
1 4-inch piece of ginger, sliced and charred	2 cinnamon sticks
4-star anise	3 cloves
2 tablespoons soy sauce	200g rice noodles
Toppings: bean sprouts, basil leaves, lime wedges, sliced chili, hoisin sauce, and Sriracha	

Instructions:

(1) Heat oven to 400°F/200°C. The eggplant slices should be tender and slightly colored after 25 minutes on a baking sheet, oiled, and rotated. **(2)** Vegetable broth, charred onion, garlic, ginger, cinnamon sticks, star anise, and cloves should all be combined in a big saucepan. After reaching a boil, lower the heat and simmer for 30 minutes. **(3)** After straining the soup and removing the solids, pour the stock back into the saucepan. Add the roasted eggplant pieces and soy sauce. Simmer for ten minutes. **(4)** Drain and set aside rice noodles after following package instructions. **(5)** Divide the noodles among dishes for serving. Over the noodles, ladle the heated combination of eggplant broth. Garnish with the suggested toppings and serve.

TEMPEH PHO

Preparation Time: 20 minutes || Cooking Time: 30 minutes || Servings: 4

Ingredients:

200g tempeh, sliced	1 liter vegetable broth
1 onion, thinly sliced	4 garlic cloves, minced
1-inch piece ginger, grated	2-star anise
1 cinnamon stick	2 tablespoons soy sauce
200g rice noodles	100g bean sprouts
2 spring onions, sliced	A handful of fresh cilantro, roughly chopped
A handful of fresh mint, roughly chopped	1 lime, cut into wedges
Chili slices, to taste Sriracha sauce to serve	Hoisin sauce to serve

Instructions:

(1) The vegetable broth should be brought to a boil in a big saucepan. Add the soy sauce, star anise, garlic, ginger, onion, and cinnamon stick. For 20 minutes, simmer over low heat to let the flavors seep into the broth. **(2)** Proceed to cook and drain the rice noodles, then set aside. **(3)** Fry the tempeh slices in a pan until they get golden brown on both sides. Put aside. **(4)** After straining the soup to get rid of the spices, put it back in the pot. Reduce the heat to a simmer once more. **(5)** Spoon cooked noodles into each of four bowls. Add bean sprouts, spring onions, cilantro, mint, and tempeh pieces on top. **(6)** Cover the noodles and toppings with the heated broth. Present the dish alongside wedges of lime, slices of Chile, hoisin sauce, and sriracha sauce.

LENTIL PHO

Preparation Time: 15 minutes || Cooking Time: 45 minutes || Servings: 4

Ingredients:

1 cup green lentils	1 liter vegetable broth
1 onion, thinly sliced	4 garlic cloves, minced
1-inch piece ginger, grated	2-star anise
1 cinnamon stick	2 tablespoons soy sauce
200g rice noodles	100g bean sprouts
2 spring onions, sliced	A handful of fresh cilantro, roughly chopped
A handful of fresh basil, roughly chopped	1 lime, cut into wedges
Chili slices, to taste Sriracha sauce to serve	Hoisin sauce to serve

Instructions:

(1) Cook lentils in boiling water for 20 minutes until soft after rinsing. Drain and set aside. **(2)** Boil vegetable broth in a big saucepan. Stir in onion, garlic, ginger, star anise, cinnamon stick, and soy sauce. Simmer on low for 20 minutes. **(3)** Follow package instructions, drain, and set aside rice noodles. **(4)** Strain and return spice-free broth to the pot. Return the stock to a boil with the cooked lentils. **(5)** Divide cooked noodles into four bowls. Add lentils, bean sprouts, spring onions, cilantro, and basil. **(6)** Pour boiling broth over noodles and toppings. Have lime wedges, Chile slices, hoisin sauce, and sriracha sauce on hand.

SPINACH PHO

Preparation Time: 15 minutes || Cooking Time: 30 minutes || Servings: 4

Ingredients:

200g fresh spinach	1 liter vegetable broth
1 onion, thinly sliced	4 garlic cloves, minced
1-inch piece ginger, grated	2-star anise
1 cinnamon stick	2 tablespoons soy sauce
200g rice noodles	100g bean sprouts
2 spring onions, sliced	A handful of fresh cilantro, roughly chopped
A handful of fresh basil, roughly chopped	1 lime, cut into wedges
Chili slices, to taste Sriracha sauce to serve	Hoisin sauce to serve

Instructions:

(1) The vegetable broth should be brought to a boil in a big saucepan. Add the soy sauce, star anise, garlic, ginger, onion, and cinnamon stick. After lowering the temperature to low, simmer for 20 minutes. **(2)** Drain and set aside rice noodles after following package instructions. **(3)** Thoroughly wash the spinach and coarsely cut it. **(4)** After straining the soup to get rid of the spices, put it back in the pot. Cook the spinach in the broth for two to three minutes or until it wilts. **(5)** Spoon cooked noodles into each of four bowls. Add wilted spinach, basil, cilantro, bean sprouts, and spring onions on top. **(6)** Cover the noodles and toppings with the heated broth. Present the dish alongside wedges of lime, slices of Chile, hoisin sauce, and sriracha sauce.

KALE PHO

Preparation Time: 15 minutes || Cooking Time: 30 minutes || Servings: 4

Ingredients:

8 cups vegetable broth	2 cups water
1 large onion, halved	4 garlic cloves, minced

and thinly sliced
2 tablespoons ginger, grated
4-star anise
1 tablespoon soy sauce
200g rice noodles
1 cup bean sprouts
Fresh cilantro for garnish
Optional: sliced chili peppers for garnish

2 cinnamon sticks
2 teaspoons coriander seeds
1 tablespoon hoisin sauce
4 cups kale, chopped
4 green onions, sliced
Lime wedges for serving

Instructions:

(1) Mix vegetable broth, water, onion, garlic, ginger, cinnamon sticks, star anise, and coriander seeds in a big saucepan. After boiling on high, decrease heat to medium, cover, and simmer for 20 minutes to infuse the broth with spices. **(2)** Return the broth to the pot after straining the solids. Mix in soy and hoisin. **(3)** Drain and set aside rice noodles after cooking them per the box. **(4)** Cook the greens in the stock for 5 minutes until soft. **(5)** Divide cooked noodles into four dishes to assemble. Cover noodles with heated broth and greens. Add bean sprouts, green onions, and cilantro. Serve with lime wedges and optional Chile peppers.

BROCCOLI PHO

Preparation Time: 15 minutes || Cooking Time: 30 minutes || Servings: 4

Ingredients:

8 cups vegetable broth
4 garlic cloves, minced
1 cinnamon stick
1 teaspoon fennel seeds
1 tablespoon miso paste
3 cups broccoli florets
1 bell pepper, thinly sliced

1 large onion, halved and thinly sliced
2 tablespoons ginger, grated
3-star anise
1 tablespoon tamari or soy sauce
200g flat rice noodles
1 cup sliced mushrooms
Fresh basil leaves for garnish

Bean sprouts, for garnish
Lime wedges for serving

Instructions:

(1) The vegetable broth, onion, garlic, ginger, cinnamon stick, star anise, and fennel seeds should all be combined in a big saucepan. Start by boiling it, then turn down the heat and let it cook for 20 minutes. **(2)** To get rid of the solids, strain the broth. Once the soup is back in the pot, thoroughly mix in the miso paste and tamari (or soy sauce). **(3)** Drain and set aside rice noodles after following package instructions. **(4)** To the broth, add the bell pepper, mushrooms, and broccoli. Simmer the veggies for five to seven minutes or until they are soft but not mushy. **(5)** Spoon cooked noodles into each of four bowls. Over the noodles, ladle the heated broth and veggies. Add bean sprouts and basil leaves as garnish, then serve with lime wedges on the side.

CAULIFLOWER PHO

Preparation Time: 15 minutes || Cooking Time: 30 minutes || Servings: 4

Ingredients:

8 cups vegetable broth
1 large onion, halved and thinly sliced
2 tablespoons ginger, grated
4-star anise
1 tablespoon soy sauce

2 cups water
4 garlic cloves, minced

2 cinnamon sticks
1 teaspoon cloves
1 tablespoon fish sauce (optional; can substitute with additional soy sauce for a vegetarian version)

200g rice noodles
1 cup carrot, julienned
Fresh cilantro for garnish
Optional: hoisin sauce and Sriracha for serving

3 cups cauliflower florets
Fresh mint leaves, for garnish
Lime wedges for serving

Instructions:

(1) Add water, vegetable broth, cloves, star anise, onion, garlic, and ginger to a big saucepan. Start by boiling it, then turn down the heat and let it cook for 20 minutes. **(2)** After straining, pour the broth back into the pot. Add the fish sauce (if used) and soy sauce and stir. **(3)** Drain and set aside rice noodles after following package instructions. **(4)** Add the carrot and cauliflower to the broth. Simmer the veggies for five to seven minutes or until they are soft. **(5)** Divide noodles into four serving bowls. Put vegetables and broth on noodles. Garnish with lime wedges, cilantro, and mint. Offer Sriracha and hoisin sauce on the side.

BELL PEPPER PHO

Preparation Time: 20 minutes || Cooking Time: 1 hour || Servings: 4

Ingredients:

8 cups vegetable broth	2 big bell peppers (1 red, 1 yellow), thinly sliced
1 large onion, thinly sliced	4 cloves garlic, minced
1 tablespoon ginger, grated	2-star anise
1 cinnamon stick	2 tablespoons soy sauce
Salt and pepper, to taste	200g rice noodles
Toppings: fresh cilantro, sliced green onions, lime wedges, bean sprouts, sliced chili	

Instructions:

(1) The vegetable broth, bell peppers, onion, garlic, ginger, star anise, and cinnamon stick should all be combined in a big saucepan. Bring over high heat to a boil. **(2)** For forty-five minutes, simmer over low heat. This enables the tastes to combine. **(3)** Remove the particles from the broth by straining it. After adding the soy sauce back to the saucepan, return the broth to it. To taste, add salt and pepper for seasoning. **(4)** As directed on the package, prepare the rice noodles. Pour out and distribute among serving dishes. **(5)** Over the noodles, pour the heated broth. Per person: Let them add sliced chili, bean sprouts, lime wedges, cilantro, green onions, and bean sprouts to their pho as they choose.

SNAP PEA PHO

Preparation Time: 15 minutes || Cooking Time: 30 minutes || Servings: 4

Ingredients:

8 cups vegetable broth	2 cups snap peas, trimmed
1 large onion, thinly sliced	4 cloves garlic, minced
1 tablespoon ginger, grated	1 lemongrass stalk, tough outer layers removed, and inner core minced
2 tablespoons fish sauce	200g rice noodles
Toppings: fresh basil leaves, sliced green onions, lime wedges, bean sprouts	

Instructions:

(1) The vegetable broth should be brought to a boil in a big saucepan. Add the minced lemongrass, onion, garlic, ginger, and snap peas. **(2)** Simmer for 20 minutes on low heat. The snap peas need to be crisp but soft. **(3)** Add the fish sauce and taste, adding more salt and pepper if needed. **(4)** After cooking the rice noodles as directed on the package, distribute them among serving dishes. **(5)** Over the noodles, ladle the heated broth and veggies. Garnish with bean sprouts, lime wedges, basil, and green onions.

CARROT PHO

Preparation Time: 20 minutes || Cooking Time: 45 minutes || Servings: 4

Ingredients:

Ingredients:

8 cups vegetable broth	Three large carrots were peeled and made into thin strips.
1 onion, thinly sliced	4 cloves garlic, minced
1 tablespoon ginger, grated	3-star anise
1 cinnamon stick	1 tablespoon soy sauce
200g rice noodles	Toppings: fresh cilantro, mint leaves, lime wedges, bean sprouts, thinly sliced radishes

Instructions:

(1) The vegetable broth, carrots, onion, garlic, ginger, star anise, and cinnamon stick should all be combined in a big saucepan. After bringing to a boil, turn down the heat. **(2)** For forty minutes, simmer. The carrots should be soft, and the liquid should be aromatic. **(3)** Empty the broth by straining out the sediments. Stir in the soy sauce after adding the stock back to the pot. To taste, add salt and pepper for seasoning. **(4)** As instructed on the packaging, prepare the rice noodles. Spoon noodles into each bowl. **(5)** Over the noodles, pour the heated broth. Garnish with bean sprouts, radishes, lime wedges, cilantro, and mint leaves.

ZUCCHINI PHO

Preparation Time: 20 minutes || Cooking Time: 30 minutes || Servings: 4 servings

Ingredients:

4 large zucchinis, spiralized or julienned	8 cups vegetable broth
2-star anise	1 cinnamon stick
3 cloves	1 cardamom pod
2-inch piece of ginger, sliced	2 garlic cloves, minced
2 tablespoons soy sauce	1 tablespoon rice vinegar
1 cup sliced mushrooms	1 carrot, thinly sliced
1 bell pepper, thinly sliced	1 block of firm tofu, cubed
Fresh herbs (cilantro, basil, mint)	Bean sprouts, lime wedges, and sliced jalapeños for serving

Instructions:

(1) Vegetable broth, star anise, cinnamon, cloves, cardamom, ginger, and garlic should all be combined in a big saucepan. **(2)** Boil and simmer the broth for 20 minutes over medium heat to infuse it with spices. **(3)** After straining the soup to get rid of the spices, put it back in the pot. Add rice vinegar and soy sauce. **(4)** Add the bell pepper, carrot, and mushrooms to the broth. Simmer for ten minutes or until the veggies are soft. **(5)** After adding the cubed tofu, simmer for a further five minutes. **(6)** The spiralized zucchini should be divided among four bowls. Over the zucchini noodles, pour the boiling broth and veggies. **(7)** Present the dish alongside freshly chopped jalapeños, bean sprouts, lime wedges, and fresh herbs.

SWEET POTATO PHO

Preparation Time: 20 minutes || Cooking Time: 40 minutes || Servings: 4 servings

Ingredients:

2 large sweet potatoes, peeled and spiralized	8 cups vegetable broth
1 onion, halved and thinly sliced	4 cloves garlic, minced
1 tablespoon grated ginger	2 cinnamon sticks
4-star anise	2 cloves
1 cardamom pod	2 tablespoons soy sauce
2 teaspoons brown sugar	1 cup shredded cabbage
1 cup thinly sliced mushrooms	1 cup bean sprouts
Tofu or cooked chicken, optional	Fresh herbs (cilantro, basil), lime wedges, and hoisin sauce for serving

Instructions:

(1) Aromatize ginger, garlic, and onion in a large pot. Add cardamom, cloves, cinnamon, and star anise. Simmer for 30 minutes after boiling. **(2)** When you're done, pour the water back into the pot. Mix in the soy sauce and brown sugar. **(3)** Add the mushrooms, cabbage, and spiralized sweet potatoes to the saucepan. Simmer for approximately ten minutes or until the sweet potatoes are soft. **(4)** Add the cooked chicken or tofu, if using, and reheat thoroughly. **(5)** Present the pho in bowls garnished with bean sprouts, chopped lime wedges, fresh herbs, and a dollop of hoisin sauce.

PUMPKIN PHO

Preparation Time: 20 minutes || Cooking Time: 45 minutes || Servings: 4 servings

Ingredients:

2 cups pumpkin, peeled and cubed	8 cups vegetable broth
1 large onion, chopped	4 garlic cloves, minced
1 tablespoon grated ginger	2 cinnamon sticks
4-star anise	2 cloves
1 cardamom pod	2 tablespoons fish sauce
1 tablespoon brown sugar	Rice noodles, cooked according to package instructions
1 cup sliced mushrooms	Bean sprouts, fresh herbs (cilantro, basil), lime wedges, and sliced chili for serving

Instructions:

(1) Fry the ginger, garlic, and onion in a big saucepan until aromatic. After adding, boil the pumpkin cubes for five minutes. **(2)** Stir in the cardamom pod, cloves, cinnamon sticks, and star anise. After bringing to a boil, simmer the pumpkin for 30 minutes or until it is soft. **(3)** Put the pumpkin chunks back in the saucepan after straining the soup and discarding the seasonings. **(4)** Add brown sugar and fish sauce (or soy sauce) and stir. Taste and adjust the seasoning. **(5)** Sliced mushrooms and cooked rice noodles should be added to the broth. Simmer for a further five minutes. **(6)** Arrange the pho in bowls and top with sliced chiles, lime wedges, fresh herbs, and bean sprouts.

BUTTERNUT SQUASH PHO

Preparation Time: 20 minutes || Cooking Time: 1 hour || Servings: 4

Ingredients:

1 butternut squash, peeled, seeded, and cubed	8 cups vegetable broth
2 cinnamon sticks	3-star anise
4 cloves	2 cardamom pods
1 large onion, quartered	4 slices ginger
2 tablespoons soy sauce	Salt and pepper, to taste
Rice noodles, cooked according to package instructions	Toppings: sliced green onions, fresh cilantro, bean sprouts, lime wedges

Instructions:

(1) The butternut squash, onion, ginger, cloves, star anise, cinnamon sticks, and cardamom pods should all be combined in a big saucepan. **(2)** After boiling, decrease the heat and cook the squash for 45 minutes until very soft. **(3)** Unspicy the soup and purée until smooth. Again, add salt, pepper, and soy sauce to the pot. **(4)** Spoon cooked rice noodles into each dish. Spoon the noodles with the butternut squash broth. **(5)** Serve with bean sprouts, lime wedges, cilantro, and green onions as garnishes on the side.

COCONUT CURRY TOFU PHO

Preparation Time: 15 minutes || Cooking Time: 30 minutes || Servings: 4

Ingredients:

1 block of firm tofu, compressed and cut into cubes	1 tablespoon oil
1 can (14 oz) coconut milk	4 cups vegetable broth
2 tablespoons curry powder	1 tablespoon soy sauce
1 tablespoon brown sugar	1 red bell pepper, sliced

1 cup mushrooms, sliced	Rice noodles, cooked according to package instructions
Toppings: basil leaves, sliced red chili, bean sprouts, lime wedges	

Instructions:

(1) In a big saucepan, warm the oil over medium heat. Fry the tofu cubes until they get golden brown. Take out and reserve the tofu. **(2)** Brown sugar, soy sauce, curry powder, coconut milk, and vegetable broth should all be added to the same pot. Give it a good stir and simmer. **(3)** Add mushrooms and red bell pepper to saucepan. Soften vegetables in 10 minutes of simmering. **(4)** Put the tofu back in the saucepan and give it a good heat. **(5)** Fill bowls with cooked rice noodles. Over the noodles, pour the tofu and coconut curry liquid. **(6)** Garnish with bean sprouts, sliced red Chile, basil leaves, and lime wedges.

THAI BASIL TOFU PHO

Preparation Time: 15 minutes || Cooking Time: 25 minutes || Servings: 4

Ingredients:

1 block of firm tofu, compressed and cut into cubes	1 tablespoon oil
4 cups vegetable broth	2 teaspoons soy sauce
1-star anise	2 cloves garlic, minced
1 inch ginger, sliced	2 green onions, chopped
1 cup Thai basil leaves	Rice noodles, cooked according to package instructions
Toppings: bean sprouts, sliced jalapeños, lime wedges, additional Thai basil leaves	

Instructions:

(1) Medium-heat oil in a large pot. Golden-fry tofu chunks. Reserve the tofu. **(2)** Add the green onions, ginger, garlic, star anise, soy sauce, and vegetable broth to the same saucepan. Simmer for around fifteen minutes. **(3)** Add the fried tofu and the Thai basil leaves. Simmer for five more minutes. **(4)** Spoon cooked rice noodles into each dish. Over the noodles, ladle the tofu and broth. **(5)** Garnish with more Thai basil leaves, bean sprouts, lime wedges, and sliced jalapeños.

LEMONGRASS-GINGER TOFU PHO

Preparation Time: 30 minutes || Cooking Time: 1 hour || Servings: 4

Ingredients:

8 cups vegetable broth	1 block of firm tofu, compressed and cut into cubes
3 stalks of lemongrass, tough outer layers removed, thinly sliced	3-inch piece of ginger, peeled and minced
2 tablespoons soy sauce	2 tablespoons rice vinegar
200g rice noodles	2 carrots, julienned
200g mushrooms, sliced	1 onion, thinly sliced
2 cloves garlic, minced	1 tablespoon vegetable oil
Fresh cilantro for garnish	Bean sprouts, for garnish
Lime wedges for serving	Hoisin sauce for serving
Sriracha, for serving	

Instructions:

(1) Heat vegetable oil in a big saucepan on medium. Slice onion, mince garlic, lemongrass, and ginger. Sauté 5 minutes until fragrant. **(2)** Pour veggie broth into the pot. After boiling, lower heat and simmer for 30 minutes to infuse flavors. **(3)** Fried cubed tofu in a separate pan until golden brown on all sides. Set aside. **(4)** Prepare rice noodles according to package instructions. **(5)** Add soy sauce and rice vinegar to soup and season to taste. **(6)** Divide cooked noodles into four dishes to serve. Add sautéed tofu, mushrooms, and carrots. **(7)** Pour the broth over noodles and toppings in each dish after straining. **(8)** Serve with bean sprouts and fresh cilantro. Serve alongside lime wedges, hoisin sauce, and Sriracha.

LEMONGRASS-CHILI TOFU PHO

Preparation Time: 25 minutes || Cooking Time: 1 hour || Servings: 4

Ingredients:

8 cups vegetable broth	1 block of firm tofu, compressed and cut into cubes
3 stalks of lemongrass, tough outer layers removed, thinly sliced	2 red chilies, seeded and finely sliced
2 tablespoons soy sauce	1 tablespoon rice vinegar
200g rice noodles	2 bell peppers, thinly sliced
1 cup snap peas	1 onion, thinly sliced
2 cloves garlic, minced	1 tablespoon vegetable oil
Fresh basil for garnish	Bean sprouts, for garnish
Lime wedges for serving	Hoisin sauce for serving
Sriracha, for serving	

Instructions:

(1) In a big saucepan, heat vegetable oil on medium. Add onion, garlic, lemongrass, and red chilies. Cook for 5 minutes until fragrant. **(2)** Add veggie broth and boil. Reduce heat and simmer for 30 minutes. **(3)** Fried tofu cubes in a separate pan until crispy and golden. Set aside. **(4)** Follow the package instructions to cook rice noodles. **(5)** Adjust flavor with soy sauce and rice vinegar in broth. **(6)** For pho, place noodles in bowls and top with tofu, bell pepper slices, and snap peas. **(7)** Pour broth over each bowl after straining. **(8)** Add fresh basil and bean sprouts. Serve alongside lime wedges, hoisin sauce, and Sriracha.

LEMONGRASS-COCONUT TOFU PHO

Preparation Time: 20 minutes || Cooking Time: 1 hour || Servings: 4

Ingredients:

8 cups vegetable broth	1 can (400ml) coconut milk
1 block of firm tofu, compressed and cut into cubes	3 stalks of lemongrass, tough outer layers removed, thinly sliced
2 tablespoons soy sauce	1 tablespoon lime juice
200g rice noodles	1 sweet potato, peeled and thinly sliced
1 cup kale, chopped	1 onion, thinly sliced
2 cloves garlic, minced	1 tablespoon vegetable oil
Fresh mint, for garnish	Bean sprouts, for garnish
Lime wedges for serving	Hoisin sauce for serving
Sriracha, for serving	

Instructions:

(1) Heat vegetable oil in a big saucepan on medium. Add onion, garlic, and lemongrass and simmer for 5 minutes until fragrant. **(2)** Put vegetable broth and coconut milk in the saucepan and boil. Lower heat and simmer for 30 minutes. **(3)** Sauté tofu cubes till crispy and golden. Set aside. **(4)** Cook rice noodles as directed on the packet. **(5)** Combine soy sauce and lime juice with broth, seasoning as needed. **(6)** Place noodles in bowls and top with tofu, sweet potato pieces, and greens to make pho. **(7)** Pour the broth over noodles and toppings in each dish after straining. **(8)** Add fresh mint and bean sprouts, then serve with lime wedges, hoisin sauce, and Sriracha.

LEMONGRASS-CILANTRO TOFU PHO

Preparation Time: 20 minutes || Cooking Time: 1 hour || Servings: 4

Ingredients:

8 cups vegetable broth	1 large onion, halved and thinly sliced
4 cloves garlic, minced	2 stalks lemongrass, tough outer layers removed, thinly sliced
1-inch piece ginger,	2-star anise

thinly sliced
1 cinnamon stick
1 block (14 oz) firm tofu, pressed and cut into cubes
1 cup cilantro, roughly chopped
Bean sprouts for serving
Sriracha sauce for serving
2 tablespoons soy sauce
200g rice noodles
2 limes, cut into wedges
Hoisin sauce for serving
Salt, to taste

Instructions:

(1) Boil vegetable broth in a big saucepan. Adding onion, garlic, lemongrass, ginger, star anise, and cinnamon stick. Simmer on low for 30 minutes to infuse the broth with flavor. **(2)** Return the broth to the pot after straining off the solids. Add soy sauce and salt to taste. **(3)** Rice noodles should be cooked in a separate pot according to the box. Reserve and drain. **(4)** Continue simmering the broth with tofu cubes for 10 minutes. **(5)** Divide cooked noodles into four bowls to make pho. Pour broth and tofu over noodles. Add cilantro, lime wedges, bean sprouts, hoisin sauce, and Sriracha to taste. **(6)** Serve hot and enjoy!

LEMONGRASS-KAFFIR LIME TOFU PHO

Preparation Time: 30 minutes || Cooking Time: 1 hour || Servings: 4 servings

Ingredients:

8 cups vegetable broth
2 stalks lemongrass, bruised
1 large onion, halved and charred
2-inch piece ginger, sliced and bruised
200g rice noodles
200g mushrooms, sliced
Toppings: Bean sprouts, lime wedges, fresh herbs (cilantro, basil), sliced chili, hoisin sauce, and Sriracha
1 block of firm tofu, compressed and cubed
6 kaffir lime leaves
4 cloves garlic, smashed
2 tablespoons soy sauce
2 carrots, thinly sliced
Salt to taste

Instructions:

(1) The vegetable broth should be brought to a boil in a big saucepan. Stir in the soy sauce, charred onion, garlic, ginger, lemongrass, and kaffir lime leaves. Allow to steep for half an hour to flavor the broth. **(2)** To the broth, add the tofu, carrots, and mushrooms. Simmer for twenty minutes more. Add salt to taste to season. **(3)** While the broth simmers, cook the rice noodles as directed. Discard after draining. **(4)** Spoon some noodles into each dish for serving. Make sure to include the tofu chunks when you ladle the boiling soup and veggies over the noodles. **(5)** Provide extras on the side so that people may personalize their Pho.

LEMONGRASS-GALANGAL TOFU PHO

Preparation Time: 30 minutes || Cooking Time: 1 hour || Servings: 4 servings

Ingredients:

8 cups vegetable broth
2 stalks lemongrass, bruised
1 large onion, halved and charred
1 cinnamon stick
2 tablespoons soy sauce
1 bunch bok choy, chopped
Toppings: Green onions, bean sprouts, lime wedges, fresh herbs (cilantro, mint), sliced chili, hoisin sauce, and Sriracha
1 block of firm tofu, compressed and cubed
2-inch piece galangal, sliced
4 cloves garlic, smashed
3-star anise
200g rice noodles
Salt to taste

Instructions:

(1) The vegetable broth should be brought to a boil in a big saucepan. Stir in the soy sauce, cinnamon, star anise, charred onion, garlic, lemongrass, and galangal. Allow to simmer for half an hour. **(2)** To the broth, add the book choy and tofu. Bok choy should be cooked for 20 minutes or until soft. Add some salt for seasoning. **(3)** Following the directions on the package, prepare the rice noodles, drain them, and divide them into bowls. **(4)** Over the noodles, ladle the tofu, broth, and book choy. To customize, serve with a range of toppings.

LEMONGRASS-THAI CHILI TOFU PHO

Preparation Time: 30 minutes || Cooking Time: 1 hour || Servings: 4 servings

Ingredients:

8 cups vegetable broth	1 block of firm tofu, compressed and cubed
2 stalks lemongrass, bruised	4 Thai chilis, sliced (adjust to taste)
1 large onion, halved and charred	4 cloves garlic, smashed
2-inch piece ginger, sliced and bruised	2 tablespoons soy sauce
200g rice noodles	2 bell peppers, thinly sliced
Salt to taste	Toppings: Bean sprouts, lime wedges, fresh herbs (cilantro, Thai basil), sliced chili, hoisin sauce, and Sriracha

Instructions:

(1) Boil vegetable broth in a big pot. Add soy sauce, ginger, garlic, charred onion, lemongrass, and Thai chilies. Simmer for 30 minutes. **(2)** Tofu and bell peppers should be added to the stew. Cook until the peppers are soft, about 20 minutes. Add salt to taste as needed. **(3)** After cooking the rice noodles as directed on the package, divide them into bowls. **(4)** Top the noodles with the tofu, veggies, and hot broth. To add personality, top with a variety of toppings before serving.

LEMONGRASS-SOY TOFU PHO

Preparation Time: 20 minutes || Cooking Time: 1 hour || Servings: 4

Ingredients:

8 cups vegetable broth	2 stalks lemongrass, chopped
1 onion, thinly sliced	4 cloves garlic, minced
1 tablespoon ginger, grated	1 tablespoon soy sauce
1 tablespoon brown sugar	1 teaspoon sesame oil
1 package of firm tofu, drain and chop	200g rice noodles
Bean sprouts, cilantro, lime wedges, and thinly sliced chili for garnish	

Instructions:

(1) The vegetable broth, lemongrass, onion, ginger, garlic, soy sauce, brown sugar, and sesame oil should all be combined in a big saucepan. **(2)** When it starts to boil, turn down the heat and let it cook for thirty minutes. **(3)** Simmer the tofu cubes in the stock for a further fifteen to twenty minutes after adding them. **(4)** As you wait, prepare the rice noodles per the directions on the box. **(5)** After the noodles are cooked, distribute them among bowls for serving. **(6)** Over the noodles, ladle the boiling broth and tofu. **(7)** Serve hot, topped with thinly sliced Chile, lime wedges, cilantro, and bean sprouts.

LEMONGRASS-FISH SAUCE TOFU PHO

Preparation Time: 25 minutes || Cooking Time: 1 hour || Servings: 4

Ingredients:

8 cups vegetable broth	2 stalks lemongrass, chopped
1 onion, thinly sliced	4 cloves garlic, minced
1 tablespoon ginger, grated	2 tablespoons fish sauce
1 tablespoon brown sugar	1 teaspoon sesame oil
1 package of firm tofu, drained, chopped	200g rice noodles

Bean sprouts, Thai basil, lime wedges, and thinly sliced chili for garnish

Instructions:

(1) The vegetable broth, fish sauce, brown sugar, sesame oil, onion, garlic, ginger, and lemongrass should all be combined in a big saucepan. **(2)** When it starts to boil, turn down the heat and let it cook for thirty minutes. **(3)** Simmer the tofu cubes in the stock for a further fifteen to twenty minutes after adding them. **(4)** As you wait, prepare the rice noodles per the directions on the box. **(5)** After the noodles are cooked, distribute them among bowls for serving. **(6)** Over the noodles, ladle the boiling broth and tofu. **(7)** Serve hot with thinly sliced Chile, lime wedges, Thai basil, and bean sprouts as garnish.

LEMONGRASS-OYSTER SAUCE TOFU PHO

Preparation Time: 30 minutes || Cooking Time: 1 hour || Servings: 4

Ingredients:

8 cups vegetable broth	2 stalks lemongrass, chopped
1 onion, thinly sliced	4 cloves garlic, minced
1 tablespoon ginger, grated	2 tablespoons oyster sauce
1 tablespoon brown sugar	1 teaspoon sesame oil
1 package of firm tofu, drained, chopped	200g rice noodles
Bean sprouts, mint leaves, lime wedges, and thinly sliced chili for garnish	

Instructions:

(1) The vegetable broth, brown sugar, sesame oil, oyster sauce, onion, ginger, garlic, and lemongrass should all be combined in a big saucepan. **(2)** When it starts to boil, turn down the heat and let it cook for thirty minutes. **(3)** Simmer the tofu cubes in the stock for a further fifteen to twenty minutes after adding them. **(4)** As you wait, prepare the rice noodles per the directions on the box. **(5)** After the noodles are cooked, distribute them among bowls for serving. **(6)** Over the noodles, ladle the boiling broth and tofu. **(7)** Serve hot, topped with thinly sliced Chile, lime wedges, bean sprouts, and mint leaves.

LEMONGRASS-HOISIN TOFU PHO

Preparation Time: 20 minutes || Cooking Time: 1 hour || Servings: 4

Ingredients:

8 cups vegetable broth	2 stalks lemongrass, tender parts only, finely chopped
200g rice noodles	400g firm tofu, pressed and cubed
2 tablespoons hoisin sauce	1 onion, sliced thinly
4 cloves garlic, minced	1-inch piece ginger, minced
2-star anise	1 cinnamon stick
2 tablespoons soy sauce	Fresh herbs (cilantro, basil)
Bean sprouts, lime wedges, and sliced chili for garnish	

Instructions:

(1) The vegetable broth should be simmered in a big saucepan. Incorporate the star anise, cinnamon stick, onion, garlic, ginger, and lemongrass. To bring out the flavors in the broth, simmer it for half an hour. **(2)** Hoisin sauce should be used to pan-sauté the tofu pieces until they become caramelized. Put aside. **(3)** As directed on the package, prepare the rice noodles. **(4)** After straining the broth to get rid of the solids, put it back in the pot. Taste and adjust seasoning, then add soy sauce. **(5)** Place some rice noodles and then tofu cubes in each dish to assemble the Pho. Over the noodles and tofu, ladle the heated broth. **(6)** As garnish, serve with bean sprouts, lime wedges, sliced chiles, and fresh herbs on the side.

LEMONGRASS-SESAME TOFU PHO

Preparation Time: 20 minutes || Cooking Time: 1 hour || Servings: 4

Ingredients:

8 cups vegetable broth	2 stalks lemongrass, tender parts only, finely chopped
200g rice noodles	400g firm tofu, pressed and cubed
2 tablespoons sesame oil	1 tablespoon soy sauce
1 onion, sliced thinly	4 cloves garlic, minced
1-inch piece ginger, minced	2-star anise
1 cinnamon stick	Fresh herbs (cilantro, mint)
Bean sprouts, lime wedges, and sliced chili for garnish	Toasted sesame seeds for garnish

Instructions:

(1) The vegetable broth should be simmered in a big saucepan. Incorporate the star anise, cinnamon stick, onion, garlic, ginger, and lemongrass. Allow to simmer for half an hour. **(2)** The tofu cubes should be marinated in soy sauce and sesame oil for ten minutes before being sautéed till golden. Put aside. **(3)** As directed on the package, prepare the rice noodles. **(4)** After straining out the solids, put the broth back into the pot. Taste and adjust the seasoning. **(5)** Place the noodles in bowls and top with the tofu to assemble the Pho. Cover the noodles and tofu with a heated broth. **(6)** Add bean sprouts, lime wedges, sliced chiles, fresh herbs, and toasted sesame seeds as garnish.

LEMONGRASS-TAMARIND TOFU PHO

Preparation Time: 20 minutes || Cooking Time: 1 hour || Servings: 4

Ingredients:

8 cups vegetable broth	2 stalks lemongrass, tender parts only, finely chopped
200g rice noodles	400g firm tofu, pressed and cubed
2 tablespoons tamarind paste	1 tablespoon soy sauce
1 onion, sliced thinly	4 cloves garlic, minced
1-inch piece ginger, minced	2-star anise
1 cinnamon stick	Fresh herbs (cilantro, Thai basil)
Bean sprouts, lime wedges, and sliced chili for garnish	

Instructions:

(1) The vegetable broth should be simmered in a big saucepan. Incorporate the star anise, cinnamon stick, onion, garlic, ginger, and lemongrass. Allow to simmer for half an hour. **(2)** Coat the tofu cubes equally with a mixture of soy sauce and tamarind paste. Cook until the sides get crunchy. Put aside. **(3)** Following the package instructions, cook the rice noodles. **(4)** After straining the broth to get rid of the solids, put it back in the saucepan. To have a tangier flavor, adjust the spice and add extra tamarind paste if preferred. **(5)** To assemble, put noodles in bowls, cover with tofu, then drizzle with heated broth. **(6)** Garnish with sliced chiles, bean sprouts, lime wedges, and fresh herbs.

LEMONGRASS-VINEGAR TOFU PHO

Preparation Time: 20 minutes || Cooking Time: 1 hour || Servings: 4

Ingredients:

8 cups vegetable broth	1 block of firm tofu, compressed and cubed
2 stalks lemongrass, minced	2 tablespoons rice vinegar
2 tablespoons soy sauce	1 teaspoon sugar
4 servings of rice noodles	1 onion, thinly sliced

2 cloves garlic, minced	1 inch ginger, grated
2-star anise	1 cinnamon stick
Fresh herbs (cilantro, basil)	Bean sprouts, lime wedges, and sliced chili for garnish

Instructions:

(1) The vegetable broth should be brought to a boil in a big saucepan. Add the cinnamon stick, star anise, ginger, garlic, and lemongrass. To infuse flavors, reduce heat and simmer for half an hour. **(2)** Tofu cubes should be sautéed in a different pan with sugar, soy sauce, and rice vinegar until golden brown. Put aside. **(3)** After cooking the rice noodles, drain and rinse with cold water. **(4)** After taking the spices out of the soup, add the onion slices. Simmer for five more minutes. **(5)** Divide the noodles among dishes for serving. Place the cooked tofu on top, cover with the heated broth, and decorate with bean sprouts, sliced Chile, lime wedges, and fresh herbs.

LEMONGRASS-CORNSTARCH TOFU PHO

Preparation Time: 20 minutes || Cooking Time: 1 hour || Servings: 4

Ingredients:

8 cups vegetable broth	1 block of firm tofu, compressed and cubed
2 tablespoons cornstarch	2 stalks lemongrass, minced
2 tablespoons soy sauce	1 teaspoon sugar
4 servings of rice noodles	1 onion, thinly sliced
2 cloves garlic, minced	1 inch ginger, grated
2-star anise	1 cinnamon stick
Fresh herbs (cilantro, basil)	Bean sprouts, lime wedges, and sliced chili for garnish

Instructions:

(1) Coat the tofu cubes well with cornstarch. **(2)** Bring the vegetable broth, star anise, garlic, ginger, lemongrass, and cinnamon stick to a boil in a big saucepan. Simmer for thirty minutes on low heat. **(3)** Crispy tofu covered with cornstarch should be pan-fried. Put aside. **(4)** Rinse and drain rice noodles after following package instructions. **(5)** After taking the spices out of the broth, simmer the onion slices for an additional five minutes. **(6)** To assemble the Pho, put noodles in bowls, add crispy tofu on top, and then pour broth over them. Add lime, chili, bean sprouts, and fresh herbs as garnish.

LEMONGRASS-BLACK BEAN TOFU PHO

Preparation Time: 20 minutes || Cooking Time: 1 hour || Servings: 4

Ingredients:

8 cups vegetable broth	1 block of firm tofu, compressed and cubed
2 tablespoons black bean sauce	2 stalks lemongrass, minced
1 tablespoon soy sauce	1 teaspoon sugar
4 servings of rice noodles	1 onion, thinly sliced
2 cloves garlic, minced	1 inch ginger, grated
2-star anise	1 cinnamon stick
Fresh herbs (cilantro, basil)	Bean sprouts, lime wedges, and sliced chili for garnish

Instructions:

(1) For fifteen minutes, marinate tofu cubes in a mixture of sugar, soy sauce, and black bean sauce. **(2)** For half an hour, simmer vegetable broth with star anise, ginger, garlic, and lemongrass. **(3)** The marinated tofu should be pan-fried until brown on all sides. **(4)** Once the rice noodles are cooked as directed, drain and rinse. **(5)** After scraping off the spices from the stock, boil the onion for an additional five minutes. **(6)** To serve, arrange noodles and tofu in bowls and top with bean sprouts, lime wedges, and chili sprigs.

LEMONGRASS-GARLIC TOFU PHO

Preparation Time: 20 minutes || Cooking Time: 1 hour || Servings: 4

Ingredients:

8 cups vegetable broth	1 block of firm tofu, compressed and cubed
4 cloves garlic, minced	2 stalks lemongrass, minced
2 tablespoons soy sauce	1 teaspoon sugar
4 servings of rice noodles	1 onion, thinly sliced
1 inch ginger, grated	2-star anise
1 cinnamon stick	Fresh herbs (cilantro, basil)
Bean sprouts, lime wedges, and sliced chili for garnish	

Instructions:

(1) For fifteen minutes, marinate tofu in a mixture of sugar, soy sauce, lemongrass, and chopped garlic. **(2)** Add the star anise, cinnamon stick, extra garlic, and ginger to the boiling vegetable soup. Allow to simmer for half an hour. **(3)** The marinated tofu should be pan-fried until browned. **(4)** Follow the directions to prepare the rice noodles, then rinse and drain. **(5)** Simmer the onion in the broth for five minutes after removing the seasonings. **(6)** To serve, divide the noodles and tofu among bowls, cover with hot broth, and top with bean sprouts, lime wedges, and Chile.

CHAPTER: 5 SEAFOOD PHO CREATIONS:

SHRIMP PHO

Preparation Time: 30 minutes || Cooking Time: 1 hour || Servings: 4

Ingredients:

1 lb large shrimp, peeled and deveined	8 cups chicken or vegetable broth
1 onion, halved and thinly sliced	4 garlic cloves, minced
1 (3-inch) piece of ginger, sliced	2-star anise
2 cinnamon sticks	4 cloves
2 tablespoons fish sauce	1 tablespoon sugar
Salt, to taste	8 oz rice noodles
Fresh herbs (cilantro, basil, mint) for garnish	Bean sprouts, for garnish
Lime wedges for garnish	Sliced jalapenos for garnish
Hoisin sauce and sriracha, for serving	

Instructions:

(1) Boil broth in a big pot. Add the cloves, cinnamon sticks, star anise, onion, garlic, and ginger. To infuse the broth with the aromatics, simmer for half an hour. **(2)** Add salt, sugar, and fish sauce to the soup to season it. After adding the shrimp to the broth, simmer it for three to five minutes or until it turns pink and opaque. **(3)** As you wait, make the rice noodles as directed on the package. **(4)** Serve the noodles in four plates. Ladle hot broth and shrimp over noodles. Garnish with jalapenos, bean sprouts, lime wedges, and herbs. Provide Sriracha and Hoisin Sauce.

CRAB PHO

Preparation Time: 45 minutes || Cooking Time: 1 hour 30 minutes || Servings: 4

Ingredients:

2 lbs crab (preferably blue crab), cleaned and quartered	8 cups seafood or vegetable broth
1 onion, halved and thinly sliced	4 garlic cloves, minced
1 (3-inch) piece of ginger, sliced	2-star anise
2 cinnamon sticks	4 cloves
2 tablespoons fish sauce	1 tablespoon sugar
Salt, to taste	8 oz rice noodles
Fresh herbs (cilantro, basil, mint) for garnish	Bean sprouts, for garnish
Lime wedges for garnish	Sliced jalapenos for garnish
Hoisin sauce and sriracha, for serving	

Instructions:

(1) Boil broth in a big pot. Add the cloves, cinnamon sticks, onion, garlic, ginger, star anise, and crab bits. To extract the flavors from the crab and aromatics, simmer for one hour. **(2)** Take out the chunks of crab from the soup. Remove and save the flesh from the shells. **(3)** To get rid of the solids, strain the broth. Put the soup back in the pot and add salt, sugar, and fish sauce to taste. Return the crab meat to the broth and fully cook it. **(4)** As directed on the package, prepare the rice noodles. **(5)** To serve, divide the noodles among bowls, cover the noodles with broth and crab meat, and top with bean sprouts, sliced jalapenos, lime wedges, and fresh herbs. Have sriracha and hoisin sauce on hand.

FISH PHO

Preparation Time: 30 minutes || Cooking Time: 45 minutes || Servings: 4

Ingredients:

1 lb firm white fish (cod or halibut), cut into bite-sized pieces	8 cups seafood or vegetable broth
1 onion, halved and thinly sliced	4 garlic cloves, minced
1 (3-inch) piece of ginger, sliced	2-star anise
2 cinnamon sticks	4 cloves
2 tablespoons fish sauce	1 tablespoon sugar
Salt, to taste	8 oz rice noodles
Fresh herbs (cilantro, basil, mint) for garnish	Bean sprouts, for garnish
Lime wedges for garnish	Sliced jalapenos for garnish
Hoisin sauce and sriracha, for serving	

Instructions:

(1) Boil broth in a big pot. Add the cloves, cinnamon sticks, star anise, onion, garlic, and ginger. To infuse the broth with the aromatics, simmer for half an hour. **(2)** Add salt, sugar, and fish sauce to the soup to season it. After adding the fish pieces to the broth, simmer for 5 to 7 minutes or until the fish is opaque and flakes readily. **(3)** As you wait, make the rice noodles as directed on the package. **(4)** Divide the noodles into four dishes for serving. Over the noodles, ladle the heated soup and fish. Add sliced jalapenos, bean sprouts, lime wedges, and fresh herbs as garnish. Provide Sriracha and Hoisin Sauce.

CLAM PHO

Preparation Time: 20 minutes || Cooking Time: 1 hour || Servings: 4

Ingredients:

8 cups clam broth	200g rice noodles
500g Manila clams, scrubbed and cleaned	1 onion, thinly sliced
3 cloves garlic, minced	1-inch piece ginger, sliced
2 tablespoons fish sauce	1 tablespoon sugar
1 teaspoon salt	1/2 teaspoon black pepper
Fresh cilantro, basil, and lime wedges	

Instructions:

(1) The clam broth should be simmered over medium heat in a big saucepan. **(2)** To the saucepan, add the ginger, minced garlic, and chopped onion. Simmer for fifteen minutes to add flavor to the broth. **(3)** As you wait, prepare the rice noodles per the directions on the box. After draining, set away. **(4)** To the boiling broth, add the cleaned clams. Cook for five to seven minutes or until the clams have opened. Throw away any unopened clams. **(5)** Add fish sauce, sugar, salt, and black pepper to season the soup. Taste and adjust the seasoning. **(6)** Spoon cooked rice noodles into individual serving dishes. Over the noodles, ladle the heated clam soup. **(7)** Add some freshly squeezed lime juice, basil, and cilantro as garnish. **(8)** Enjoy the subtle taste of the clam pho when it's hot!

SCALLOP PHO

Preparation Time: 25 minutes || Cooking Time: 40 minutes || Servings: 4

Ingredients:

8 cups chicken or vegetable broth	200g rice noodles
500g fresh scallops, cleaned	1 onion, thinly sliced
3 cloves garlic, minced	1-inch piece ginger, sliced
2 tablespoons fish sauce	1 tablespoon soy sauce
1 teaspoon sugar	1/2 teaspoon salt
1/2 teaspoon white pepper	Bean sprouts, sliced scallions, and Thai basil for garnish

Instructions:

(1) The chicken or vegetable broth should be simmered over medium heat in a large saucepan. **(2)** To the saucepan, add the ginger, minced garlic, and chopped onion. Give it a 15-minute simmer to bring out the flavor. **(3)** Cook rice noodles per package instructions. Set aside after draining. **(4)** Clean scallops and add to boiling broth. Cook scallops for 3–4 minutes until just done. **(5)** Add fish sauce, soy sauce, sugar, salt, and white pepper to season the soup. Taste and adjust the seasoning. **(6)** Spoon cooked rice noodles into individual serving dishes. Over the noodles, ladle the heated scallop soup. **(7)** Add bean sprouts, Thai basil, and sliced scallions as garnish. **(8)** Serve hot and enjoy the subtle sweetness of the Pho with scallops!

LOBSTER PHO

Preparation Time: 30 minutes || Cooking Time: 50 minutes || Servings: 4

Ingredients:

8 cups lobster or seafood broth	200g rice noodles
2 lobster tails, shells removed, and meat sliced	1 onion, thinly sliced
3 cloves garlic, minced	1-inch piece ginger, sliced
2 tablespoons fish sauce	1 tablespoon hoisin sauce
1 teaspoon sugar	1/2 teaspoon salt
1/2 teaspoon sriracha (optional)	Fresh cilantro, mint, and lime wedges for garnish

Instructions:

(1) The lobster or seafood stock should be simmered over medium heat in a large saucepan. **(2)** To the saucepan, add the ginger, minced garlic, and chopped onion. Simmer for fifteen minutes to add flavor to the broth. **(3)** Cook rice noodles per package instructions. Set aside after draining. **(4)** Sliced lobster flesh should be added to the boiling stock. Cook the lobster for five to seven minutes or until it is cooked through and opaque. **(5)** Add fish sauce, hoisin sauce, sugar, salt, and, if desired, Sriracha to season the soup. Taste and adjust the seasoning. **(6)** Spoon cooked rice noodles into individual serving dishes. Over the noodles, ladle the heated lobster broth. **(7)** Add some fresh mint, cilantro, and lime juice as garnish. **(8)** Serve hot and savor the opulent tastes of the lobster pho!

SQUID PHO

Preparation Time: 20 minutes || Cooking Time: 1 hour || Servings: 4

Ingredients:

8 cups beef or vegetable broth	250g dried rice noodles
300g squid, cleaned and sliced	1 onion, thinly sliced
3 cloves garlic, minced	1 thumb-sized piece of ginger, sliced
2-star anise	2 cinnamon sticks
3 cloves	1 tablespoon fish sauce
1 tablespoon soy sauce	1 tablespoon sugar
Salt and pepper to taste	Fresh herbs (cilantro, Thai basil, mint) for garnish

Bean sprouts, lime wedges, and chili slices for serving

Instructions:

(1) Bring the broth (either beef or veggie) to a boil in a big saucepan. **(2)** Add the cloves, cinnamon sticks, star anise, onion, garlic, and ginger. To infuse flavors, simmer for thirty minutes. **(3)** As you wait, soften the rice noodles by soaking them in boiling water per the directions on the box, then drain. **(4)** Pour sugar, soy sauce, and fish sauce into the soup. Add salt and pepper to taste. **(5)** When the squid is cooked, add it to the stock and boil for two to three minutes. **(6)** Divide the rice noodles into serving dishes to serve. Over the noodles, ladle the heated broth and squid. **(7)** Add bean sprouts, lime wedges, sliced chilies, and fresh herbs as garnish. Enjoy while hot!

OCTOPUS PHO

Preparation Time: 30 minutes || Cooking Time: 1 hour 30 minutes || Servings: 4

Ingredients:

8 cups seafood or vegetable broth	250g dried rice noodles
300g octopus, cleaned and sliced	1 onion, thinly sliced
3 cloves garlic, minced	1 thumb-sized piece of ginger, sliced
2-star anise	2 cinnamon sticks
3 cloves	1 tablespoon fish sauce
1 tablespoon soy sauce	1 tablespoon sugar
Salt and pepper to taste	Fresh herbs (cilantro, Thai basil, mint) for garnish
Bean sprouts, lime wedges, and chili slices for serving	

Instructions:

(1) The seafood or vegetable broth should be brought to a boil in a big saucepan. **(2)** Add the cloves, cinnamon sticks, star anise, onion, garlic, and ginger. To infuse flavors, simmer for forty-five minutes. **(3)** As you wait, soften the rice noodles by soaking them in boiling water per the directions on the box, then drain. **(4)** Pour sugar, soy sauce, and fish sauce into the soup. Add salt and pepper to taste. **(5)** When the octopus is cooked, add it to the stock and simmer it for one hour. **(6)** Divide the rice noodles into serving dishes to serve. Over the noodles, ladle the heated broth and octopus. **(7)** Add bean sprouts, lime wedges, sliced chilies, and fresh herbs as garnish. Enjoy while hot!

MUSSEL PHO

Preparation Time: 25 minutes || Cooking Time: 45 minutes || Servings: 4

Ingredients:

8 cups seafood or vegetable broth	250g dried rice noodles
500g mussels, cleaned and debearded	1 onion, thinly sliced
3 cloves garlic, minced	1 thumb-sized piece of ginger, sliced
2-star anise	2 cinnamon sticks
3 cloves	1 tablespoon fish sauce
1 tablespoon soy sauce	1 tablespoon sugar
Salt and pepper to taste	Fresh herbs (cilantro, Thai basil, mint) for garnish
Bean sprouts, lime wedges, and chili slices for serving	

Instructions:

(1) The seafood or vegetable broth should be brought to a boil in a big saucepan. **(2)** Add the cloves, cinnamon sticks, star anise, onion, garlic, and ginger. For 20 minutes, simmer to infuse flavors. **(3)** As you wait, soften the rice noodles by soaking them in boiling water per the directions on the box, then drain. **(4)** Pour sugar, soy sauce, and fish sauce into the soup. Add salt and pepper to taste. **(5)** Once in the liquid, add the mussels and boil for 5 to 7 minutes or until they open. **(6)** After taking the mussels out of their shells, set them aside. **(7)** Divide the rice noodles into serving dishes to serve. Spoon the steaming liquid onto the noodles and place the mussels on top. **(8)** Add bean sprouts, lime wedges, sliced chilies, and fresh herbs as garnish. Enjoy while hot!

MIXED SEAFOOD PHO

Preparation Time: 30 minutes || Cooking Time: 1 hour || Servings: 4

Ingredients:

8 cups chicken or vegetable broth	1 large onion, halved and unpeeled
4 cloves garlic, unpeeled	1 (4-inch) piece ginger, halved lengthwise
2-star anise	2 cinnamon sticks
1 teaspoon coriander seeds	1 tablespoon fish sauce
1 tablespoon sugar	1 teaspoon salt
8 ounces rice noodles	1-pound mixed seafood (shrimp, scallops, squid)
2 cups bean sprouts	Fresh herbs (cilantro, basil, mint)
Lime wedges for serving	Sliced chili for serving
Hoisin sauce and Sriracha for serving	

Instructions:

(1) Start blackening the onion, garlic, and ginger in a big saucepan over medium heat for 5 minutes. **(2)** Stir in the coriander seeds, cinnamon sticks, star anise, and broth. **(3)** When it starts to boil, turn down the heat and let it cook for thirty minutes. **(4)** After straining, put the broth back in the saucepan and add the salt, sugar, and fish sauce. **(5)** After cooking the rice noodles as directed on the package, divide them into bowls and drain. **(6)** After bringing the broth to a boil, add the mixed seafood and simmer for two to three minutes or until it is just done. **(7)** Over the noodles, ladle the heated broth and seafood. Present the dish alongside bean sprouts, fresh herbs, sliced chiles, lime wedges, and sauces.

COCONUT CURRY SHRIMP PHO

Preparation Time: 20 minutes || Cooking Time: 30 minutes || Servings: 4

Ingredients:

1 tablespoon oil	1 small onion, finely chopped
2 cloves garlic, minced	1 tablespoon freshly grated ginger
2 tablespoons red curry paste	4 cups chicken or vegetable broth
1 can (14 ounces) coconut milk	1 tablespoon fish sauce
1 tablespoon sugar	8 ounces rice noodles
1 pound shrimp, peeled and deveined	2 cups bean sprouts
Fresh cilantro and lime wedges for serving	

Instructions:

(1) Melt oil in a pot on medium. Simmer onion, garlic, and ginger for 5 minutes to soften. **(2)** After approximately a minute, stir in the curry paste until aromatic. **(3)** Stir in the sugar, fish sauce, coconut milk, and broth. Simmer and cook for fifteen minutes. **(4)** After cooking the rice noodles as directed on the package, divide them into bowls and drain. **(5)** Add shrimp to simmering broth and cook for 3–4 minutes until pink and opaque. **(6)** Drizzle the noodles with the broth and shrimp. Accompany with lime wedges, cilantro, and bean sprouts.

THAI BASIL SHRIMP PHO

Preparation Time: 20 minutes || Cooking Time: 25 minutes || Servings: 4

Ingredients:

8 cups chicken or vegetable broth	1 stalk lemongrass, removed stiff outer layers and bruised stalk
1 (4-inch) piece ginger, halved	2 cloves garlic, smashed

lengthwise
2 tablespoons fish sauce
1 teaspoon salt
1 pound shrimp, peeled and deveined
1 cup fresh Thai basil leaf
Sliced chili for serving

1 tablespoon sugar
8 ounces rice noodles
2 cups bean sprouts
Lime wedges for serving

Instructions:

(1) Bring the broth, ginger, garlic, and lemongrass to a boil in a big saucepan. Simmer for 20 minutes on low heat. **(2)** Using a slotted spoon, remove the ginger, garlic, and lemongrass from the liquid. Add salt, sugar, and fish sauce and stir. **(3)** After cooking the rice noodles as directed on the package, divide them into bowls and drain. **(4)** Add shrimp to simmering broth and cook for 3–4 minutes until pink and opaque. **(5)** Drizzle the noodles with the broth and shrimp. Add bean sprouts, sliced Chile, lime wedges, and Thai basil on top.

LEMONGRASS-GINGER SHRIMP PHO

Preparation Time: 30 minutes || Cooking Time: 1 hour || Servings: 4

Ingredients:

1 stalk lemongrass, minced
1 lb (450g) shrimp, peeled and deveined
200g rice noodles

1 tablespoon sugar
2 green onions, sliced
Fresh herbs (cilantro, basil)
Salt and pepper to taste

1 inch ginger, grated
8 cups (2L) chicken or vegetable broth
2 tablespoons fish sauce
2 cloves garlic, minced
1 cup bean sprouts
2 limes, quartered
Chili slices (optional for garnish)

Instructions:

(1) Add the garlic, ginger, lemongrass, and vegetable or chicken broth to a big saucepan. To infuse flavors, bring to a boil, then lower heat and simmer for 20 minutes. **(2)** After adding the shrimp to the stock, heat for two to three minutes or until they become pink. Take out the prawns and place them aside. **(3)** Add sugar, salt, pepper, and fish sauce to the soup to season it. Make adjustments based on your preference. **(4)** Drain rice noodles after cooking them according to the box. **(5)** Divide the noodles into dishes to assemble. Ladle heated broth over shrimp and place them on top. **(6)** If preferred, garnish with bean sprouts, green onions, lime wedges, fresh herbs, and chili slices. **(7)** Enjoy your Lemongrass-Ginger Shrimp Pho while it's still hot.

LEMONGRASS-CHILI SHRIMP PHO

Preparation Time: 30 minutes || Cooking Time: 1 hour || Servings: 4

Ingredients:

1 stalk lemongrass, minced
1 lb (450g) shrimp, peeled and deveined
200g rice noodles
1 tablespoon sugar
2 green onions, sliced
Fresh herbs (cilantro, basil)
Salt and pepper to taste

1-2 red chilies, sliced
8 cups (2L) chicken or vegetable broth
2 tablespoons fish sauce
2 cloves garlic, minced
1 cup bean sprouts
2 limes, quartered

Instructions:

(1) Add the garlic, chiles, lemongrass, and vegetable or chicken broth to a big saucepan. After bringing to a boil, simmer for twenty minutes. **(2)** Cook the shrimp in the broth until they become pink. Take out the prawns and place them aside. **(3)** Add sugar, salt, pepper, and fish sauce to the soup to season it. **(4)** Prepare rice noodles per package instructions and set aside. **(5)** Pour hot broth over noodles and shrimp that have been divided into bowls to assemble the pho. **(6)** Add lime wedges, bean sprouts, fresh herbs, and green onions as garnish. **(7)** Enjoy your Lemongrass-Chili Shrimp Pho right away after serving.

LEMONGRASS-COCONUT SHRIMP PHO

Preparation Time: 30 minutes || Cooking Time: 1 hour || Servings: 4

Ingredients:

1 stalk lemongrass, minced	1 can (400ml) coconut milk
1 lb (450g) shrimp, peeled and deveined	6 cups (1.5L) chicken or vegetable broth
200g rice noodles	2 tablespoons fish sauce
1 tablespoon sugar	2 cloves garlic, minced
2 green onions, sliced	1 cup bean sprouts
Fresh herbs (cilantro, basil)	2 limes, quartered
Salt and pepper to taste	

Instructions:

(1) Garlic, lemongrass, coconut milk, and chicken or vegetable broth should all be combined in a big saucepan. After bringing to a boil, simmer for twenty minutes. **(2)** Cook the shrimp in the saucepan until they take on a pink hue. Take out the prawns and place them aside. **(3)** Add sugar, salt, pepper, and fish sauce to the soup to season it. **(4)** Drain the rice noodles after cooking them per the packet. **(5)** To serve, arrange noodles in dishes, top with shrimp, then cover with hot broth. **(6)** Add lime wedges, bean sprouts, fresh herbs, and green onions as garnish. **(7)** Savor the smooth and velvety Coconut-Lemongrass Shrimp Pho.

LEMONGRASS-CILANTRO SHRIMP PHO

Preparation Time: 30 minutes || Cooking Time: 1 hour || Servings: 4

Ingredients:

8 cups chicken or vegetable broth	2 stalks lemongrass, tender inner white parts only, chopped
1-inch piece ginger, sliced	2 cloves garlic, minced
2 tablespoons fish sauce	1 teaspoon sugar
200g rice noodles	400g shrimp, peeled and deveined
1 cup cilantro leaves, roughly chopped	2 limes, cut into wedges
2 jalapeños, thinly sliced	1 cup bean sprouts
Salt to taste	

Instructions:

(1) In a big pot, boil broth. Add sugar, fish sauce, ginger, garlic, and lemongrass. Simmer 20 minutes to blend flavors. **(2)** After straining, pour the broth back into the pot. Return to a simmer. **(3)** After cooking the rice noodles as directed on the package, divide them into four bowls and drain. **(4)** The shrimp should be pink and cooked in 3–4 minutes in the boiling liquid. **(5)** Over the noodles in the bowls, pour the shrimp and boiling broth. **(6)** Add bean sprouts, jalapeños, lime wedges, and cilantro to the top of each bowl. **(7)** Present the dish hot, letting each guest taste and adjust the flavor with salt.

LEMONGRASS-MINT SHRIMP PHO

Preparation Time: 30 minutes || Cooking Time: 1 hour || Servings: 4

Ingredients:

8 cups chicken or vegetable broth	2 stalks lemongrass, tender inner white parts only, chopped
1-inch piece ginger, sliced	2 cloves garlic, minced
2 tablespoons fish sauce	1 teaspoon sugar
200g rice noodles	400g shrimp, peeled and deveined
1 cup mint leaves, roughly chopped	2 limes, cut into wedges
2 jalapeños, thinly sliced	1 cup bean sprouts
Salt to taste	

Instructions:

(1) In a big pot, boil broth. Add sugar, fish sauce, ginger, garlic, and lemongrass. Simmer the broth for 20 minutes to enhance the taste. **(2)** After straining, pour the broth back into the pot. Return to a simmer. **(3)** After cooking the rice noodles as directed on the package, divide them into four bowls and drain. **(4)** Put the shrimp in the boiling broth and simmer for 3–4 minutes until pink and done. **(5)** Over the noodles in the bowls, pour the shrimp and boiling broth. **(6)** Add bean sprouts, lime wedges, jalapeños, and mint to the top of each bowl. **(7)** Serve right away, letting each guest add more salt to taste as required.

LEMONGRASS-BASIL SHRIMP PHO

Preparation Time: 30 minutes || Cooking Time: 1 hour || Servings: 4

Ingredients:

8 cups chicken or vegetable broth	2 stalks lemongrass, tender inner white parts only, chopped
1-inch piece ginger, sliced	2 cloves garlic, minced
2 tablespoons fish sauce	1 teaspoon sugar
200g rice noodles	400g shrimp, peeled and deveined
1 cup basil leaves, roughly chopped	2 limes, cut into wedges
2 jalapeños, thinly sliced	1 cup bean sprouts
Salt to taste	

Instructions:

(1) In a big pot, boil broth. Add sugar, fish sauce, ginger, garlic, and lemongrass. Simmer 20 minutes to blend flavors. **(2)** After straining, pour the broth back into the pot. Return to a simmer. **(3)** After cooking the rice noodles as directed on the package, divide them into four bowls and drain. **(4)** When the stock is simmering, add the shrimp and cook for 3 to 4 minutes or until they are pink and cooked through. **(5)** Over the noodles in the bowls, pour the shrimp and boiling broth. **(6)** Add bean sprouts, lime wedges, jalapeños, and basil to each bowl as garnish. **(7)** Present the food hot and let each guest add salt according to their preference.

LEMONGRASS-KAFFIR LIME SHRIMP PHO

Preparation Time: 30 minutes || Cooking Time: 1 hour || Servings: 4

Ingredients:

1 tablespoon vegetable oil	2 stalks lemongrass, finely chopped
6 kaffir lime leaves, torn	1 onion, thinly sliced
2 liters of chicken or vegetable broth	1 teaspoon sugar
2 tablespoons fish sauce	200g rice noodles
400g shrimp, peeled and deveined	200g bean sprouts
Fresh herbs (cilantro, basil)	Lime wedges for serving
Chili slices for serving	

Instructions:

(1) Heat the vegetable oil in a big saucepan over medium heat. Incorporate the onion, kaffir lime leaves, and lemongrass. For approximately five minutes, or until the onion is transparent, sauté. **(2)** Add broth after sugar and fish sauce. To let flavors soak in, decrease the heat and simmer the broth for 45 minutes after boiling. **(3)** Meanwhile, follow the directions on the package to make the rice noodles. After draining, set away. **(4)** Cook the shrimp in the broth for three to five minutes or until they become pink. **(5)** Divide the noodles into four bowls and assemble. Drizzle the noodles with the broth and shrimp. Add bean sprouts, chopped chilies, lime wedges, and fresh herbs on top. **(6)** Enjoy the fragrant combination of kaffir lime and lemongrass when served hot.

LEMONGRASS-GALANGAL SHRIMP PHO

Preparation Time: 30 minutes || Cooking Time: 1 hour || Servings: 4

Ingredients:

1 tablespoon vegetable oil	2 stalks lemongrass, finely chopped
4 slices galangal	1 onion, thinly sliced
2 liters of chicken or	1 teaspoon sugar

vegetable broth

2 tablespoons fish sauce	200g rice noodles
400g shrimp, peeled and deveined	200g bean sprouts
Fresh herbs (cilantro, mint)	Lime wedges for serving
Chili slices for serving	

Instructions:

(1) A large pot of oil should be heated over medium heat. Incorporate ginger, onion, and lemongrass. Soften the onion. **(2)** Incorporate the fish sauce, sugar, and broth. Simmer for forty-five minutes after bringing to a simmer. **(3)** The packaging should tell you how to cook rice noodles. Remove. **(4)** Once in the broth, add the shrimp and simmer until they become pink. **(5)** Place the noodles, broth, shrimp, bean sprouts, cilantro, lime, and Chile into the bowls and assemble. **(6)** This bowl of comfort is a unique combination of galangal and lemongrass.

LEMONGRASS-THAI CHILI SHRIMP PHO

Preparation Time: 30 minutes || Cooking Time: 1 hour || Servings: 4

Ingredients:

1 tablespoon vegetable oil	2 stalks lemongrass, finely chopped
2 Thai chilis, sliced	1 onion, thinly sliced
2 liters of chicken or vegetable broth	1 teaspoon sugar
2 tablespoons fish sauce	200g rice noodles
400g shrimp, peeled and deveined	200g bean sprouts
Fresh herbs (cilantro, Thai basil)	Lime wedges for serving
Extra chili slices for serving	

Instructions:

(1) Oil in a saucepan over medium heat. Onion, chilies, and lemongrass. Simmer onion till tender. **(2)** Add fish sauce and sugar after adding the stock. Allow to simmer for forty-five minutes. **(3)** Separately cook the rice noodles and leave them aside. **(4)** Cook the shrimp by adding them to the broth. **(5)** Spoon noodles into bowls, top with bean sprouts, herbs, lime, and Chile, then pour over broth with shrimp. **(6)** Present the dish right away, delivering a spicily aromatic bite with every bite.

LEMONGRASS-SOY SHRIMP PHO

Preparation Time: 20 minutes || Cooking Time: 45 minutes || Servings: 4

Ingredients:

1 tablespoon vegetable oil	2 stalks lemongrass, finely chopped
1 onion, thinly sliced	4 cloves garlic, minced
1-inch piece of ginger, sliced	6 cups chicken or vegetable broth
2 tablespoons soy sauce	1 teaspoon sugar
1 pound shrimp, peeled and deveined	200g rice noodles
Garnishes: bean sprouts, thinly sliced green onions, fresh cilantro, lime wedges	

Instructions:

(1) Heat the vegetable oil in a big saucepan over medium heat. Add the ginger, garlic, onion, and lemongrass. After around five minutes of sautéing, the onion should be tender and aromatic. **(2)** Boil after adding broth. Simmer sugar and soy sauce for 30 minutes to blend flavors. **(3)** Add pink, completely cooked shrimp to the pot and boil for 3–5 minutes. **(4)** As you wait, make the rice noodles as directed on the package. **(5)** Spoon cooked noodles into each of four bowls. Over the noodles, ladle the heated broth and shrimp. Present the garnishes separately so that guests may customize them to their taste.

LEMONGRASS-FISH SAUCE SHRIMP PHO

Preparation Time: 20 minutes || Cooking Time: 45 minutes || Servings: 4

Ingredients:

1 tablespoon vegetable oil	2 stalks lemongrass, finely chopped
1 onion, thinly sliced	4 cloves garlic, minced
1-inch piece of ginger, sliced	6 cups chicken or vegetable broth
2 tablespoons fish sauce	1 teaspoon sugar
1 pound shrimp, peeled and deveined	200g rice noodles
Garnishes: basil leaves, thinly sliced red chili, lime wedges	

Instructions:

(1) Place the oil in a big saucepan and heat it over medium heat. Ginger, garlic, onion, and lemongrass should be added. Cook the onion until it becomes transparent. **(2)** After adding the broth, simmer. After adding the sugar and fish sauce, simmer for a further half hour. **(3)** When the shrimp are pink and well cooked, add them and cook. **(4)** Follow the steps on the box to cook the rice noodles. **(5)** Serve the noodles in dishes with the broth and shrimp on top, garnished with lime wedges, red chili flakes, and basil leaves.

LEMONGRASS-OYSTER SAUCE SHRIMP PHO

Preparation Time: 20 minutes || Cooking Time: 45 minutes || Servings: 4

Ingredients:

1 tablespoon vegetable oil	2 stalks lemongrass, finely chopped
1 onion, thinly sliced	4 cloves garlic, minced
1-inch piece of ginger, sliced	6 cups chicken or vegetable broth
2 tablespoons oyster sauce	1 teaspoon sugar
1 pound shrimp, peeled and deveined	200g rice noodles
Garnishes: sliced mushrooms, Bok choy leaves, green onions, lime wedges	

Instructions:

(1) Warm oil in a large pot on medium. Lemongrass, garlic, ginger, and onion soften the onion. **(2)** Add the oyster sauce, sugar, and broth. To allow the flavors to meld, simmer for half an hour. **(3)** When the shrimp are pink, add them to the stew and simmer. **(4)** To make rice noodles, follow the package instructions. **(5)** To serve, sort the noodles into bowls, pour in the shrimp soup, and top with the lime wedges, book choy, green onions, and mushrooms.

LEMONGRASS-HOISIN SHRIMP PHO

Preparation Time: 20 minutes || Cooking Time: 45 minutes || Servings: 4

Ingredients:

1 tablespoon vegetable oil	2 stalks lemongrass, finely chopped
1 onion, thinly sliced	4 cloves garlic, minced
1-inch piece of ginger, sliced	6 cups chicken or vegetable broth
2 tablespoons hoisin sauce	1 pound shrimp, peeled and deveined
200g rice noodles	Garnishes: bean sprouts, thinly sliced green onions, fresh cilantro, lime wedges, hoisin sauce for drizzling

Instructions:

(1) In a big saucepan, warm the oil over medium heat. Add the ginger, garlic, onion, and lemongrass. The onion should be sautéed until transparent. **(2)** Simmer after adding the broth. After 30 minutes of simmering, stir in the hoisin sauce. **(3)** When the shrimp are cooked through and pink, add them to the saucepan. **(4)** As directed on the package, prepare the rice noodles. **(5)** Place the noodles in the dishes and top with the broth and shrimp to assemble the pho. Garnish and serve with more hoisin sauce on the side.

LEMONGRASS-SESAME SHRIMP PHO

Preparation Time: 20 minutes || Cooking Time: 45 minutes || Servings: 4

Ingredients:

1 tablespoon vegetable oil	2 stalks lemongrass, finely chopped
1 onion, thinly sliced	4 cloves garlic, minced
1-inch piece of ginger, sliced	6 cups chicken or vegetable broth
2 tablespoons sesame oil	1 pound shrimp, peeled and deveined
200g rice noodles	Garnishes: sesame seeds, thinly sliced green onions, fresh cilantro, lime wedges

Instructions:

(1) Medium-heat oil in a large pot. Simmer ginger, garlic, onion, and lemongrass. **(2)** After adding the broth, boil the mixture. After adding the sesame oil, simmer for an additional thirty minutes. **(3)** Cook the shrimp until they become pink and are well done. **(4)** Simply follow the directions on the package to cook the rice noodles. **(5)** Spoon noodles and pho into bowls; top with shrimp and broth. Add lime wedges, cilantro, green onions, and sesame seeds as garnish.

LEMONGRASS-TAMARIND SHRIMP PHO

Preparation Time: 20 minutes || Cooking Time: 45 minutes || Servings: 4

Ingredients:

1 tablespoon vegetable oil	2 stalks lemongrass, finely chopped
1 onion, thinly sliced	4 cloves garlic, minced
1-inch piece of ginger, sliced	6 cups chicken or vegetable broth
2 tablespoons tamarind paste	1 teaspoon sugar (optional; adjust to taste)
1 pound shrimp, peeled and deveined	200g rice noodles
Garnishes: bean sprouts, fresh mint leaves, thinly sliced red chili, lime wedges	

Instructions:

(1) Set the pot on medium heat and add the oil. It should smell good to have ginger, garlic, onion, and lemongrass. **(2)** After adding the broth, cook it. To mix the flavors, boil the tamarind paste (and sugar, if using) for 30 minutes after stirring. **(3)** Add the prawns and heat until they become pink. **(4)** To make rice noodles, follow the package instructions. **(5)** To serve, divide the noodles among bowls, top with the shrimp soup, and decorate with lime wedges, bean sprouts, mint leaves, and red chiles.

LEMONGRASS-VINEGAR SHRIMP PHO

Preparation Time: 20 minutes || Cooking Time: 45 minutes || Servings: 4

Ingredients:

1 tablespoon vegetable oil	2 stalks lemongrass, finely chopped
1 onion, thinly sliced	4 cloves garlic, minced
1-inch piece of ginger, sliced	6 cups chicken or vegetable broth
2 tablespoons rice vinegar	1 teaspoon sugar
1 pound shrimp, peeled and deveined	200g rice noodles
Garnishes: fresh cilantro, sliced jalapenos, lime wedges, bean sprouts	

Instructions:

(1) In a big saucepan, warm the oil over medium heat. Ginger, garlic, onion, and lemongrass should be added and sautéed until the onions are tender. **(2)** After adding the broth, boil the mixture. After adding the sugar and rice vinegar, simmer for thirty minutes. **(3)** Cook the shrimp until they become pink and are well done. **(4)** As directed on the package, prepare the rice noodles. **(5)** To serve, put noodles in bowls, pour broth and shrimp over them, then serve with garnishes on the side.

LEMONGRASS-CORNSTARCH SHRIMP PHO

Preparation Time: 25 minutes || Cooking Time: 50 minutes || Servings: 4

Ingredients:

- 1 tablespoon vegetable oil
- 1 onion, thinly sliced
- 1-inch piece of ginger, sliced
- 1 tablespoon cornstarch (dilute in 2 tablespoons water)
- 1 pound shrimp, peeled and deveined
- 2 stalks lemongrass, finely chopped
- 4 cloves garlic, minced
- 6 cups chicken or vegetable broth
- 1 teaspoon sugar
- 200g rice noodles

Garnishes: green onions, sliced basil leaves, lime wedges

Instructions:

(1) Oil in a saucepan over medium heat. Incorporate ginger, garlic, onion, and lemongrass. Clear the onion by simmering. **(2)** Simmer after adding the broth. Stir in the sugar and cornstarch slurry, then boil for 35 minutes to thin up the broth a little. **(3)** Add the prawns and boil them through. **(4)** Follow the directions for cooking the rice noodles. **(5)** To assemble, add noodles to bowls, cover with shrimp broth and top with preferred garnishes.

LEMONGRASS-BLACK BEAN SHRIMP PHO

Preparation Time: 20 minutes || Cooking Time: 45 minutes || Servings: 4

Ingredients:

- 1 tablespoon vegetable oil
- 1 onion, thinly sliced
- 1-inch piece of ginger, sliced
- 2 tablespoons fermented black bean sauce
- 1 pound shrimp, peeled and deveined
- 2 stalks lemongrass, finely chopped
- 4 cloves garlic, minced
- 6 cups chicken or vegetable broth
- 1 teaspoon sugar
- 200g rice noodles

Garnishes: red chili pepper slices, chopped cilantro, lime wedges

Instructions:

(1) Oil in a saucepan over medium heat. Stir in ginger, garlic, onion, and lemongrass until fragrant. **(2)** Add sugar, sugar sauce, and broth; simmer for 30 minutes to let flavors meld. **(3)** When the shrimp become pink, add them and fry. **(4)** Do what the package says to make the rice noodles. **(5)** To serve, put noodles in dishes, top with broth and shrimp, then garnish with desired ingredients.

LEMONGRASS-GARLIC SHRIMP PHO

Preparation Time: 20 minutes || Cooking Time: 45 minutes || Servings: 4

Ingredients:

- 1 tablespoon vegetable oil
- 6 cloves garlic, minced
- 1 onion, thinly sliced
- 1 pound shrimp, peeled and deveined
- 2 tablespoons fish sauce
- 2 stalks lemongrass, finely chopped
- 1-inch piece of ginger, sliced
- 6 cups chicken or vegetable broth
- 200g rice noodles
- 1 teaspoon sugar

Garnishes: fresh cilantro, sliced green onions, bean sprouts, lime wedges

Instructions:

(1) In a big saucepan, warm the oil over medium heat. Add the onion, ginger, garlic, and lemongrass; sauté the combination until it becomes aromatic, and the onion becomes transparent. **(2)** After adding the broth, boil the mixture. After adding sugar and fish sauce, simmer for 30 minutes. **(3)** After adding the shrimp to the saucepan, simmer it for three to five minutes or until it is pink and cooked through. **(4)** As directed on the package, prepare the rice noodles. **(5)** To serve, put noodles in bowls, pour broth and shrimp over them, then serve with garnishes on the side.

LEMONGRASS-ONION SHRIMP PHO

Preparation Time: 20 minutes || Cooking Time: 45 minutes || Servings: 4

Ingredients:

- 1 tablespoon vegetable oil
- 2 onions, one thinly sliced and one chopped
- 1-inch piece of ginger, sliced
- 1 pound shrimp, peeled and deveined
- 2 tablespoons soy sauce
- 2 stalks lemongrass, finely chopped
- 4 cloves garlic, minced
- 6 cups chicken or vegetable broth
- 200g rice noodles
- 1 teaspoon sugar
- Garnishes: fresh basil, sliced jalapeños, bean sprouts, lime wedges

Instructions:

(1) Place the oil in a big saucepan and heat it over medium heat. Add the chopped onion, garlic, ginger, and lemongrass; sauté until the onion is tender. **(2)** Bring the saucepan to a simmer after adding the sugar, soy sauce, and broth. Give it a 30-minute simmer. **(3)** Add the finely sliced onion and sauté the shrimp until they turn pink and become opaque. **(4)** As you wait, make the rice noodles according to the package's instructions. **(5)** Spoon noodles into bowls, pour shrimp soup over top, then top with desired toppings.

LEMONGRASS-CARROT SHRIMP PHO

Preparation Time: 25 minutes || Cooking Time: 50 minutes || Servings: 4

Ingredients:

- 1 tablespoon vegetable oil
- 1 onion, thinly sliced
- 1-inch piece of ginger, sliced
- 6 cups chicken or vegetable broth
- 200g rice noodles
- 2 stalks lemongrass, finely chopped
- 4 cloves garlic, minced
- 2 large carrots, peeled and thinly sliced
- 1 pound shrimp, peeled and deveined
- 2 tablespoons hoisin sauce
- 1 teaspoon sugar
- Garnishes: mint leaves, sliced red chili, lime wedges, bean sprouts

Instructions:

(1) In a big saucepan, warm the oil over medium heat. Add the carrots, onion, garlic, ginger, and lemongrass; sauté the veggies until they are tender. **(2)** After adding the broth, boil the mixture. After adding the sugar and hoisin sauce, simmer for thirty-five minutes. **(3)** When the shrimp are cooked through and become pink, add them to the saucepan. **(4)** Simply follow the directions on the package to cook the rice noodles. **(5)** To serve, arrange noodles in bowls, pour in shrimp soup, then top with bean sprouts, chiles, lime wedges, and mint leaves.

LEMONGRASS-BROCCOLI SHRIMP PHO

Preparation Time: 25 minutes || Cooking Time: 50 minutes || Servings: 4

Ingredients:

- 1 tablespoon vegetable oil
- 1 onion, thinly sliced
- 1-inch piece of ginger, sliced
- 1 pound shrimp, peeled and deveined
- 200g rice noodles
- 1 teaspoon sugar
- 2 stalks lemongrass, finely chopped
- 4 cloves garlic, minced
- 6 cups chicken or vegetable broth
- 2 cups broccoli florets
- 2 tablespoons fish sauce
- Garnishes: lime wedges, fresh basil leaves, sliced green onions

Instructions:

(1) In a big saucepan, heat oil on medium. Combine lemongrass, onion, garlic, and ginger and simmer until transparent. **(2)** Add broth and simmer. Add fish sauce and sugar; simmer for 30 minutes. **(3)** I added broccoli and cooked it for three minutes, but it still had a crunchy texture. **(4)** When you add the shrimp to the pan, let it cook for three to five minutes until it's pink and done. **(5)** Prepare rice noodles according to package instructions. **(6)** To serve, place noodles in bowls, ladle the shrimp, broccoli, and broth over, and add garnishes as desired.

LEMONGRASS-CAULIFLOWER SHRIMP PHO

Preparation Time: 20 minutes || Cooking Time: 45 minutes || Servings: 4

Ingredients:

1 tablespoon vegetable oil	2 stalks lemongrass, finely chopped
1 onion, thinly sliced	4 cloves garlic, minced
1-inch piece of ginger, sliced	6 cups chicken or vegetable broth
1 pound shrimp, peeled and deveined	2 cups cauliflower florets
200g rice noodles	2 tablespoons soy sauce
1 teaspoon sugar	Garnishes: cilantro, sliced jalapeños, lime wedges

Instructions:

(1) Moderately heat oil in a big saucepan. Lemongrass, onion, garlic, and ginger sauté till aromatic. **(2)** Add broth and simmer. Add soy sauce and sugar; simmer 30 minutes. **(3)** Stir in the cauliflower and cook for about 5 minutes, until slightly tender. **(4)** Put in the shrimp and cook them until they turn pink and are done. **(5)** To prepare rice noodles, follow the package instructions. **(6)** Serve by placing noodles in bowls, adding the shrimp and cauliflower broth, and garnishing with cilantro, jalapeños, and lime wedges.

LEMONGRASS-BELL PEPPER SHRIMP PHO

Preparation Time: 20 minutes || Cooking Time: 40 minutes || Servings: 4

Ingredients:

1 tablespoon vegetable oil	2 stalks lemongrass, finely chopped
1 onion, thinly sliced	4 cloves garlic, minced
1-inch piece of ginger, sliced	6 cups chicken or vegetable broth
1 pound shrimp, peeled and deveined	1 red bell pepper, thinly sliced
1 yellow bell pepper, thinly sliced	200g rice noodles
2 tablespoons oyster sauce	1 teaspoon sugar
Garnishes: bean sprouts, fresh mint, lime wedges	

Instructions:

(1) Oil in a saucepan over medium heat. Sauté lemongrass, onion, garlic, and ginger until tender. **(2)** Add broth and bring to a simmer. Incorporate the oyster sauce and sugar; simmer for 25 minutes. **(3)** Cook the bell peppers for 5 minutes until **(4)** soft. **(5)** Add the prawns and stir them in. Cook until they are pink and done. **(6)** Prepare rice noodles according to package directions. **(7)** To serve, place noodles in bowls, pour over the shrimp and bell pepper broth and garnish with bean sprouts, mint, and lime wedges.

LEMONGRASS-SNAP PEA SHRIMP PHO

Preparation Time: 20 minutes || Cooking Time: 45 minutes || Servings: 4

Ingredients:

1 tablespoon vegetable oil	2 stalks lemongrass, finely chopped
1 onion, thinly sliced	4 cloves garlic, minced
1-inch piece of ginger, sliced	6 cups chicken or vegetable broth
1 pound shrimp, peeled and deveined	200g rice noodles
2 cups snap peas, ends trimmed	2 tablespoons fish sauce
1 teaspoon sugar	Garnishes: fresh mint leaves, thinly sliced red chili, lime wedges, bean sprouts

Instructions:

(1) Moderately heat oil in a big saucepan. Add lemongrass, onion, garlic, and ginger and sauté until transparent. **(2)** Simmer broth. To mix flavors, add fish sauce and sugar and cook for 30 minutes. **(3)** Add the shrimp and snap peas to the pot, cooking for about 3-5 minutes, until the shrimp are pink and fully cooked, and the snap peas are tender yet crisp. **(4)** Make rice noodles as directed on the box. **(5)** Serve by placing noodles in bowls, ladling the shrimp, snap peas, and broth over, and adding garnishes as desired.

LEMONGRASS-ZUCCHINI SHRIMP PHO

Preparation Time: 20 minutes || Cooking Time: 45 minutes || Servings: 4

Ingredients:

1 tablespoon vegetable oil	2 stalks lemongrass, finely chopped
1 onion, thinly sliced	4 cloves garlic, minced
1-inch piece of ginger, sliced	6 cups chicken or vegetable broth
1 pound shrimp, peeled and deveined	200g rice noodles
2 medium zucchinis, sliced into half-moons	2 tablespoons soy sauce
1 teaspoon sugar	Garnishes: basil leaves, sliced green onions, lime wedges, chili flakes

Instructions:

(1) Oil a big saucepan on medium heat. Lemongrass, onion, garlic, and ginger fry till onion softens. **(2)** Bring water to a boil in a pot. Put in the soy sauce and sugar, and let it cook for 30 minutes. **(3)** Introduce the shrimp and zucchini to the pot, cooking until the shrimp are pink and the zucchini is tender, approximately 3-5 minutes. **(4)** Prepare the rice noodles as per the package's directions. **(5)** To serve, distribute noodles among bowls, pour the shrimp, zucchini, and broth over, and offer garnishes for personalization.

LEMONGRASS-SWEET POTATO SHRIMP PHO

Preparation Time: 20 minutes || Cooking Time: 60 minutes || Servings: 4

Ingredients:

1 tablespoon vegetable oil	2 stalks lemongrass, finely chopped
1 onion, thinly sliced	4 cloves garlic, minced
1-inch piece of ginger, sliced	6 cups chicken or vegetable broth
1 large sweet potato, chunks about 1/2 inch across and peeled	1 pound shrimp, peeled and deveined
200g rice noodles	2 tablespoons fish sauce
1 teaspoon sugar	Garnishes: fresh cilantro, sliced green onions, lime wedges, diced red bell pepper

Instructions:

(1) Moderately heat oil in a big saucepan. Cook onion, garlic, ginger, lemongrass, and onion till tender. **(2)** The broth should simmer. After adding the sweet potato cubes, fish sauce, and sugar, simmer for 30–40 minutes to tenderize. **(3)** Simmer shrimp in a saucepan for 3-5 minutes until pink. **(4)** While the soup simmers, prepare the rice noodles according to the package instructions. **(5)** Serve by placing noodles in bowls, ladling the shrimp, sweet potatoes, and broth over them, and adding garnishes to taste.

LEMONGRASS-PUMPKIN SHRIMP PHO

Preparation Time: 20 minutes || Cooking Time: 60 minutes || Servings: 4

Ingredients:

1 tablespoon vegetable oil	2 stalks lemongrass, finely chopped
1 onion, thinly sliced	4 cloves garlic, minced
1-inch piece of ginger, sliced	6 cups chicken or vegetable broth
2 cups pumpkin, peeled and 1/2-inch cubes	1 pound shrimp, peeled and deveined
200g rice noodles	2 tablespoons soy sauce
1 teaspoon sugar	Garnishes: fresh basil leaves, thinly sliced chili, lime wedges, bean sprouts

Instructions:

(1) Oil a big saucepan on medium heat. Lemongrass, onion, garlic, and ginger should be translucent. **(2)** Pour in the broth, adding the cubed pumpkin, soy sauce, and sugar. Simmer for about 30-40 minutes or until the pumpkin is soft and tender. **(3)** Add the shrimp to the pot, cooking until they turn pink and are fully cooked, which should take about 3-5 minutes. **(4)** Meanwhile, make the rice noodles per the box. **(5)** To serve, distribute noodles among the bowls, pour the shrimp, pumpkin, and broth over, and offer the garnishes for individual customization.

CHAPTER: 6 REGIONAL PHO STYLES:

NORTHERN STYLE BEEF PHO (PHỞ BẮC)

Preparation Time: 30 minutes || Cooking Time: 2 hours || Servings: 4

Ingredients:

2 lbs beef bones (with marrow)	1 lb beef brisket
1 onion, halved and unpeeled	1 4-inch piece of ginger, halved lengthwise
2 cinnamon sticks	3-star anise
3 cloves	2 cardamom pods
1 tablespoon salt	3 tablespoons fish sauce
8 cups water	200g flat rice noodles
Garnishes: green onions (chopped), cilantro (chopped), lime wedges, fresh chili	

Instructions:

(1) Broil or grill onion and ginger until slightly browned. Rinse soot away. **(2)** Add brisket, beef bones, charred onion, ginger, spices, salt, fish sauce, and water to a big saucepan. First, boil, then simmer. Skim scum. **(3)** Simmer for 1.5 to 2 hours or until the brisket is tender. Remove the brisket, slice thinly, and set aside. Strain the broth, discarding solids. **(4)** Prepare rice noodles according to package instructions. **(5)** To serve, divide noodles among bowls, add slices of brisket, and ladle hot broth over. Serve with garnishes on the side.

SOUTHERN STYLE BEEF PHO (PHỞ NAM)

Preparation Time: 30 minutes || Cooking Time: 2 hours || Servings: 4

Ingredients:

2 lbs beef bones	1 lb beef brisket
1 onion, halved and unpeeled	1 4-inch piece of ginger, halved lengthwise
5-star anise	1 cinnamon stick
4 cloves	1 tablespoon sugar
3 tablespoons fish sauce	8 cups water
200g flat rice noodles	Garnishes: bean sprouts, basil leaves, lime wedges, sliced onions, hoisin sauce, sriracha

Instructions:

(1) Broil or grill onion and ginger until slightly browned. Rinse soot away. **(2)** Mix beef bones, brisket, charred onion, ginger, spices, sugar, fish sauce, and water in a big saucepan. Boil, then simmer, scraping scum. **(3)** After 1.5 to 2 hours, remove the brisket, slice thinly, and strain the broth. **(4)** Prepare rice noodles as directed. **(5)** Serve noodles and brisket in bowls, pour hot broth over, and offer a wide array of garnishes characteristic of Southern style, allowing for customization at the table.

CENTRAL STYLE BEEF PHO (PHỞ TRUNG)

Preparation Time: 30 minutes || Cooking Time: 2 hours || Servings: 4

Ingredients:

2 lbs beef bones	1 lb beef shank
1 onion, halved and unpeeled	1 4-inch piece of ginger, halved lengthwise

2 lemongrass stalks, bruised	3-star anise
1 cinnamon stick	1 tablespoon salt
2 tablespoons fish sauce	8 cups water
200g flat rice noodles	Garnishes: lime wedges, sliced onions, chopped cilantro, and mint leaves

Instructions:

(1) Char onion, ginger, and lemongrass as in previous recipes. **(2)** Place beef bones, beef shank, charred ingredients, spices, salt, fish sauce, and water in a large pot. Bring to a boil, then simmer, removing any scum. **(3)** After 1.5 to 2 hours, remove the beef shank, slice thinly, and strain the broth. **(4)** Prepare rice noodles according to instructions. **(5)** Assemble bowls with noodles, beef shank slices, and broth. Serve with garnishes that highlight the aromatic and slightly spicier broth typical of Central Vietnam.

HANOI STYLE BEEF PHO (PHỞ HÀ NỘI)

Preparation Time: 30 minutes || Cooking Time: 2 hours || Servings: 4

Ingredients:

2 lbs beef bones (preferably marrow and knuckle bones)	1 lb beef brisket
1 onion, unpeeled and quartered	1 4-inch piece of ginger, halved
3-star anise	2 cinnamon sticks
4 cloves	1 cardamom pod
1 tablespoon salt	3 tablespoons fish sauce
8 cups water	200g flat rice noodles (banh pho)
Garnishes: thinly sliced green onions, cilantro, lime wedges, fresh chili peppers	

Instructions:

(1) Burn or broil the onion and ginger until slightly charred. This deepens the broth. **(2)** Add brisket, beef bones, charred onion, ginger, spices, salt, fish sauce, and water to a big saucepan. First, boil, then simmer. Scum **(3)** should be skimmed. **(4)** The brisket should be tender after 2 hours of simmering. After cooling, slice the brisket thinly. **(5)** Strain the broth and discard the solids. Return the broth to the pot and keep it warm. **(6)** Drain rice noodles after cooking according to package directions. **(7)** To serve, divide noodles among bowls, top with slices of brisket, and ladle hot broth over. Serve with garnishes on the side.

HOI AN STYLE BEEF PHO (PHỞ HỘI AN)

Preparation Time: 30 minutes || Cooking Time: 2 hours || Servings: 4

Ingredients:

2 lbs beef bones	1 lb beef brisket
1 onion, unpeeled and quartered	1 4-inch piece of ginger, halved
1 cinnamon stick	4-star anise
3 cloves	1 cardamom pod
2 tablespoons fish sauce	1 tablespoon sugar
1 teaspoon salt	8 cups water
200g flat rice noodles (banh pho)	Garnishes: thinly sliced green onions, cilantro, lime wedges, fresh chili slices, and a pinch of ground black pepper

Instructions:

(1) Burn or broil the onion and ginger until slightly charred. **(2)** Add beef bones, brisket, charred onion, ginger, spices, fish sauce, sugar, salt, and water to a big saucepan. Heat to boiling, then simmer. Skim **(3)** surface scum. **(4)** The brisket should be tender after 2 hours of simmering. After cooling, slice the brisket thinly. **(5)** Strain the broth and discard the solids. Return the broth to the pot and keep it warm. **(6)** Drain rice noodles after cooking according to package directions. **(7)** To serve, divide noodles among bowls, top with slices of brisket, and ladle hot broth over. Serve with garnishes on the side.

NHA TRANG STYLE BEEF PHO (PHỞ NHA TRANG)

Preparation Time: 30 minutes || Cooking Time: 2 hours || Servings: 4

Ingredients:

2 lbs beef bones	1 lb beef brisket
1 onion, unpeeled and quartered	1 4-inch piece of ginger, halved
3-star anise	2 cinnamon sticks
4 cloves	2 tablespoons fish sauce
1 tablespoon sugar	1 teaspoon salt
8 cups water	200g flat rice noodles (banh pho)
1 stalk lemongrass, bruised	Garnishes: lime wedges, fresh chili slices, basil, and mung bean sprouts

Instructions:

(1) Slightly blacken the onion and ginger by grilling them over an open flame or under the broiler. **(2)** A large pot should contain beef bones, brisket, ginger, charred onion, spices, fish sauce, sugar, salt, water, and lemongrass. Turn down the heat after boiling. Remove surface scum. **(3)** Simmer until the brisket is tender, about 2 hours. Take out the brisket, allow it to cool, and then thinly slice. **(4)** Remove the particles from the broth by straining it. Bring the broth back to a simmer and cover. **(5)** After cooking the rice noodles as directed on the package, drain. **(6)** When ready to serve, divide the noodles among bowls, place beef pieces on top, and pour hot broth over. Garnishes are served on the side.

VUNG TAU STYLE BEEF PHO (PHỞ VŨNG TÀU)

Preparation Time: 30 minutes || Cooking Time: 2 hours || Servings: 4

Ingredients:

2 lbs beef bones	1 lb beef brisket
1 lb beef meatballs	1 onion, unpeeled and quartered
1 4-inch piece of ginger, halved	5-star anise
3 cinnamon sticks	1 tablespoon coriander seeds
2 tablespoons fish sauce	2 tablespoons sugar
1 teaspoon salt	8 cups water
200g flat rice noodles	Garnishes: thinly sliced onions, cilantro, lime wedges, fresh chili, and sawtooth herb

Instructions:

(1) To prepare the broth and char it, start by following the directions in Recipe 1. **(2)** For a deeper taste and texture, add the beef meatballs and brisket to the saucepan. **(3)** Once it has simmered, thinly slice the brisket and make the noodles according to the recipe. **(4)** Present the pho with its distinctive garnishes with noodles, meatballs, and chunks of beef.

PHAN THIET STYLE BEEF PHO (PHỞ PHAN THIẾT)

Preparation Time: 30 minutes || Cooking Time: 2 hours || Servings: 4

Ingredients:

2 lbs beef bones	1 lb beef brisket
1 onion, unpeeled and quartered	1 4-inch piece of ginger, halved
4-star anise	2 cinnamon sticks
6 black peppercorns	2 tablespoons fish sauce
1 tablespoon palm sugar (or brown sugar)	1 teaspoon salt
8 cups water	200g flat rice noodles
1 tablespoon dried shrimp (optional for added umami)	Garnishes: banana blossom (thinly sliced), basil, lime wedges, and fresh chili

Instructions:

(1) As said before, char the onion and ginger. **(2)** To give the soup a taste reminiscent of the shore, mix all the ingredients, including the dried shrimp if used, in a big saucepan. **(3)** Strain and assemble the pho once the meats and noodles have been prepared and simmered according to the earlier instructions. **(4)** To bring out the taste of Phan Thief, serve with the specified garnishes.

MEKONG DELTA STYLE BEEF PHO (PHỞ ĐỒNG BẰNG SÔNG CỬU LONG)

Preparation Time: 30 minutes || Cooking Time: 2 hours || Servings: 4

Ingredients:

2 lbs beef bones	1 lb beef brisket
1 onion, unpeeled and quartered	1 4-inch piece of ginger, halved
3-star anise	2 cinnamon sticks
4 cloves	2 tablespoons fish sauce
1 tablespoon palm sugar	1 teaspoon salt
8 cups water	200g flat rice noodles (banh pho)
Garnishes: lime wedges, bean sprouts, fresh herbs (mint, basil), thinly sliced chili, and banana blossom	

Instructions:

(1) Burn or broil the onion and ginger until slightly charred. **(2)** Add beef bones, brisket, charred onion, ginger, spices, fish sauce, palm sugar, salt, and water to a big saucepan. Heat to boiling, then simmer. Skim surface scum. **(3)** Simmer for 2 hours to tenderize brisket. Leave the brisket to cool, then slice thinly. **(4)** Strain broth and discard solids. Keep the broth heated in the pot. **(5)** Drain rice noodles after cooking according to package directions. **(6)** Serve noodles in dishes with beef chunks and heated broth. Serve with banana flower garnishes, a Mekong Delta specialty.

CENTRAL HIGHLANDS STYLE BEEF PHO (PHỞ TÂY NGUYÊN)

Preparation Time: 30 minutes || Cooking Time: 2.5 hours || Servings: 4

Ingredients:

2 lbs beef bones	1 lb beef brisket
1 large, sweet potato, peeled and cubed	1 onion, unpeeled and quartered
1 4-inch piece of ginger, halved	3-star anise
2 cinnamon sticks	5 black peppercorns
2 tablespoons fish sauce	1 tablespoon sugar
1 teaspoon salt	8 cups water
200g flat rice noodles	Garnishes: cilantro, green onions, lime wedges, and roasted peanuts

Instructions:

(1) As in previous recipes, char onion and ginger. **(2)** Mix everything except sweet potato in a big saucepan. Skim scum as indicated and simmer. **(3)** Add sweet potato to the broth in the last 30 minutes for a Central Highlands specialty. **(4)** The brisket should be finely sliced after cooking. Put the noodles together and make pho. **(5)** For crunch, garnish with toasted peanuts.

QUY NHON STYLE BEEF PHO (PHỞ QUY NHƠN)

Preparation Time: 30 minutes || Cooking Time: 2 hours || Servings: 4

Ingredients:

2 lbs beef bones	1 lb beef brisket
1 lb fresh seafood (such as shrimp or squid, optional)	1 onion, unpeeled and quartered
1 4-inch piece of ginger, halved	4-star anise
2 cinnamon sticks	2 lemongrass stalks, bruised
2 tablespoons fish sauce	1 tablespoon sugar
1 teaspoon salt	8 cups water

200g flat rice noodles	Garnishes: lime wedges, fresh herbs (mint, basil), thinly sliced chili, and bean sprouts

Instructions:

(1) Start by charring onion and ginger. Mix beef bones, brisket, onion, ginger, spices, fish sauce, sugar, salt, and water in a big saucepan. **(2)** Simmer as directed with lemongrass for Quy Nhon's taste. **(3)** Seafood should be added to broth in the last 5 minutes. **(4)** After simmering, thinly slice the beef, heat the noodles, and construct the pho. **(5)** Serve with fresh Quy Nhon garnishes for a land-sea taste combination.

BAC LIEU STYLE BEEF PHO (PHỞ BẠC LIÊU)

Preparation Time: 30 minutes || Cooking Time: 2 hours || Servings: 4

Ingredients:

2 lbs beef bones	1 lb beef brisket
1 lb small clams, cleaned (a unique Bac Lieu touch)	1 onion, unpeeled and quartered
1 4-inch piece of ginger, halved	4-star anise
2 cinnamon sticks	3 cloves
2 tablespoons fish sauce	1 tablespoon palm sugar
1 teaspoon salt	8 cups water
200g flat rice noodles (banh pho)	Garnishes: lime wedges, finely chopped scallions, cilantro, and sliced red chili

Instructions:

(1) Burn or broil the onion and ginger until slightly charred. **(2)** Add beef bones, brisket, charred onion, ginger, spices, fish sauce, palm sugar, salt, and water to a big saucepan. Heat to boiling, then simmer. Skim surface scum. **(3)** Simmer for 2 hours to tenderize brisket. Add cleaned clams to the pot 30 minutes before the soup is done to open. **(4)** Eliminate brisket and clams. Thinly slice brisket. Unopened clams are discarded. **(5)** Strain broth and discard solids. Keep the broth heated in the pot. **(6)** Drain rice noodles after cooking according to package directions. **(7)** Divide noodles into dishes, add beef and clam slices, then pour heated broth over. Serve with side garnishes.

VINH LONG STYLE BEEF PHO (PHỞ VĨNH LONG)

Preparation Time: 30 minutes || Cooking Time: 2 hours || Servings: 4

Ingredients:

2 lbs beef bones	1 lb beef brisket
1 pineapple, peeled and cut into chunks	1 onion, unpeeled and quartered
1 4-inch piece of ginger, halved	4-star anise
2 cinnamon sticks	3 cloves
2 tablespoons fish sauce	1 tablespoon sugar
1 teaspoon salt	8 cups water
200g flat rice noodles	Garnishes: bean sprouts, basil leaves, lime wedges, and thinly sliced onions

Instructions:

(1) Start by charring onion and ginger. **(2)** In a large saucepan, boil all ingredients except pineapple as suggested, scraping off scum. **(3)** In the last 30 minutes, add pineapple pieces to the broth for sweetness. **(4)** After cooking, thinly slice the brisket, drain the broth, and make noodles. **(5)** Add beef pieces, pineapple, noodles, hot broth, and traditional garnishes to pho.

HA LONG STYLE BEEF PHO (PHỞ HẠ LONG)

Preparation Time: 30 minutes || Cooking Time: 2 hours || Servings: 4

Ingredients:

2 lbs beef bones	1 lb beef brisket
1 lb fresh seafood (such as squid or	1 onion, unpeeled and quartered

prawns, reflecting Ha Long's coastal location)

1 4-inch piece of ginger, halved	4-star anise
2 cinnamon sticks	2 tablespoons fish sauce
1 tablespoon sugar	1 teaspoon salt
8 cups water	200g flat rice noodles

Garnishes: lime wedges, fresh herbs (mint, cilantro), thinly sliced chili, and bean sprouts

Instructions:

(1) Char onion and ginger like in previous recipes. **(2)** Mix beef bones, brisket, onion, ginger, spices, fish sauce, sugar, salt, and water in a big saucepan. Simmer, as indicated, skimming scum. **(3)** Put cleaned seafood in the saucepan for the last 10 minutes to cook. **(4)** Brisket and seafood should be removed, sliced thinly, and noodles prepared as directed. **(5)** Ha Long-inspired pho includes noodles, beef pieces, seafood, spicy broth, and garnishes.

HAI PHONG STYLE BEEF PHO (PHỞ HẢI PHÒNG)

Preparation Time: 30 minutes || Cooking Time: 2 hours || Servings: 4

Ingredients:

2 lbs beef bones	1 lb beef brisket
1 onion, unpeeled and quartered	1 4-inch piece of ginger, halved
4-star anise	2 cinnamon sticks
3 cloves	1 black cardamom pod
2 tablespoons fish sauce	1 tablespoon sugar
1 teaspoon salt	8 cups water
200g flat rice noodles (banh pho)	Garnishes: sliced red chili, chopped green onions, cilantro, lime wedges, and fried shallots

Instructions:

(1) Burn or broil the onion and ginger until slightly charred. **(2)** Add beef bones, brisket, charred onion, ginger, spices, fish sauce, sugar, salt, and water to a big saucepan. Heat to boiling, then simmer. Skim surface scum. **(3)** Simmer for 2 hours to tenderize brisket. Leave the brisket to cool, then slice thinly. **(4)** Strain broth and discard solids. Keep the broth heated in the pot. **(5)** Drain rice noodles after cooking according to package directions. **(6)** Serve noodles in dishes with beef chunks and heated broth. Hai Phong specialty garnishes include fried shallots.

DONG THAP STYLE BEEF PHO (PHỞ ĐỒNG THÁP)

Preparation Time: 30 minutes || Cooking Time: 2 hours || Servings: 4

Ingredients:

2 lbs beef bones	1 lb beef brisket
1 lotus root, peeled and sliced (a regional ingredient)	1 onion, unpeeled and quartered
1 4-inch piece of ginger, halved	4-star anise
2 cinnamon sticks	2 tablespoons fish sauce
1 tablespoon sugar	1 teaspoon salt
8 cups water	200g flat rice noodles

Garnishes: bean sprouts, basil leaves, lime wedges, and thinly sliced onions

Instructions:

(1) As in the last recipe, char the ginger and onion. **(2)** Beef bones, brisket, onion, ginger, spices, fish sauce, sugar, salt, and water should all be combined in a big saucepan. As instructed, simmer, scraping off any scum. **(3)** In the final half hour of simmering, add the sliced lotus root to the saucepan. **(4)** Once it has simmered, thinly slice the brisket, drain the broth, and make the noodles according to the recipe. **(5)**

Serve the pho hot with traditional garnishes, lotus root, noodles, and slices of beef.

SOC TRANG STYLE BEEF PHO (PHỞ SÓC TRĂNG)

Preparation Time: 30 minutes || Cooking Time: 2 hours || Servings: 4

Ingredients:

- 2 lbs beef bones
- 1 lb beef tripe, thinly sliced
- 1 4-inch piece of ginger, halved
- 3 cinnamon sticks
- 2 tablespoons fish sauce
- 1 teaspoon salt
- 200g flat rice noodles
- 1 lb beef brisket
- 1 onion, unpeeled and quartered
- 5-star anise
- 1 teaspoon black peppercorns
- 1 tablespoon palm sugar
- 8 cups water
- Garnishes: lime wedges, fresh herbs (mint, cilantro), thinly sliced chili, and bean sprouts

Instructions:

(1) Start by searing the ginger and onion. **(2)** Add the beef bones, brisket, onion, ginger, fish sauce, palm sugar, salt, and water to a big saucepan. Proceed as usual with the simmering and skimming out any scum. **(3)** Slice the beef tripe thinly and add it to the broth during the last hour of simmering. **(4)** Take out the meats, cut the brisket into thin slices, and make the noodles according to the recipe. **(5)** To enjoy pho in the Soc Trang manner, serve it with tripe, brisket, noodles, and hot broth, along with the garnishes.

TRA VINH STYLE BEEF PHO (PHỞ TRÀ VINH)

Preparation Time: 30 minutes || Cooking Time: 2 hours || Servings: 4

Ingredients:

- 2 lbs beef bones
- 1 lb beef meatballs
- 1 4-inch piece of ginger, halved
- 2 cinnamon sticks
- 2 tablespoons fish sauce
- 1 teaspoon salt
- 200g flat rice noodles (banh pho)
- 1 lb beef brisket
- 1 onion, unpeeled and quartered
- 4-star anise
- 3 cloves
- 1 tablespoon coconut sugar (a Tra Vinh touch)
- 8 cups water
- Garnishes: fresh herbs (basil, mint), bean sprouts, lime wedges, and sliced chilies

Instructions:

(1) Start by gently blackening the onion and ginger over an open flame or under a broiler. **(2)** Beef bones, brisket, onion, ginger, star anise, cinnamon, cloves, fish sauce, coconut sugar, salt, and water should all be combined in a big saucepan. **(3)** Reduce heat and simmer after boiling. Skim scum from the surface. **(4)** Add the beef meatballs to the stew and cook for an additional 45 minutes. **(5)** When the brisket is cooked, remove it, let it cool, and then thinly slice it. **(6)** After straining the broth to get rid of the solids, put it back in a clean saucepan to stay warm. **(7)** After cooking the rice noodles as directed on the package, drain. **(8)** To serve, divide the noodles among bowls, top with the meatballs and brisket pieces, and pour the boiling broth over. Garnish with parsley and serve.

BAC NINH STYLE BEEF PHO (PHỞ BẮC NINH)

Preparation Time: 30 minutes || Cooking Time: 2.5 hours || Servings: 4

Ingredients:

- 2 lbs beef bones
- 1 lb beef tendons
- 1 4-inch piece of ginger, halved
- 3 cinnamon sticks
- 2 tablespoons fish sauce
- 1 teaspoon salt
- 200g flat rice noodles
- 1 lb beef shank
- 1 onion, unpeeled and quartered
- 5-star anise
- 1 black cardamom
- 1 tablespoon rock sugar
- 8 cups water
- Garnishes: green

onions, cilantro, lime wedges, and sawtooth herb

Instructions:

(1) As said before, char the onion and ginger. **(2)** In a large saucepan, combine the charred onion, ginger, spices, fish sauce, rock sugar, salt, and water. Add the beef bones, shank, and tendons. Simmer until the shank and tendons are soft, scraping off any scum. **(3)** Cut the tendons into bite-sized pieces, remove the meats, and thinly slice the shank. **(4)** After straining the broth, reheat it. **(5)** Prepare rice noodles according to the packet. **(6)** Place the noodles, shank slices, and tendons in the bowls. After adding the heated broth, garnish and serve.

BAC GIANG STYLE BEEF PHO (PHỞ BẮC GIANG)

Preparation Time: 30 minutes || Cooking Time: 2 hours || Servings: 4

Ingredients:

2 lbs beef bones	1 lb beef brisket
1 chicken, whole (for a mix of beef and chicken broth)	1 onion, unpeeled and quartered
1 4-inch piece of ginger, halved	4-star anise
2 cinnamon sticks	3 cloves
2 tablespoons fish sauce	1 tablespoon sugar
1 teaspoon salt	8 cups water
200g flat rice noodles	Garnishes: thinly sliced onions, chopped cilantro, lime wedges, and fresh chilies

Instructions:

(1) Grill the ginger and onion. **(2)** Add the brisket, entire chicken, charred onion, ginger, sugar, salt, fish sauce, spices, and water to a big saucepan. As scum builds, remove it by simmering after bringing it to a boil. **(3)** After cooking for 30 to 40 minutes, take the chicken out of the saucepan, allow it to cool, and then shred the flesh. **(4)** After the brisket is soft, boil the broth for a further few minutes and thinly slice it. **(5)** After straining the broth and removing the solids, put it back in the saucepan. **(6)** After cooking the noodles according to the recipe, combine the noodles, shredded chicken, and pieces of brisket to make the pho. Spoon heated stock over, then top with garnishes.

LEMONGRASS-KAFFIR LIME SHRIMP PHO

Preparation Time: 30 minutes || Cooking Time: 1 hour || Servings: 4 servings

Ingredients:

1 tablespoon vegetable oil	2 stalks lemongrass, tender parts only, finely chopped
6 kaffir lime leaves, torn	1 large onion, halved and thinly sliced
2 cloves garlic, minced	6 cups chicken or vegetable broth
1-pound large shrimp, peeled and deveined	200 grams of rice noodles
2 tablespoons fish sauce	Salt, to taste
1 lime, juiced	Fresh cilantro for garnish
Bean sprouts, for garnish	Thinly sliced red chili for garnish
Lime wedges for serving	

Instructions:

(1) In a big saucepan, heat vegetable oil on medium. Incorporate lemongrass, kaffir lime leaves, onion, and garlic. Cook onions for 5 minutes, stirring regularly, until transparent. **(2)** Put the broth in and simmer. Keep the heat low and simmer for 30 minutes to blend flavors. **(3)** Set aside the rice noodles after cooking them according to the box. **(4)** Strain the soup to remove lemongrass, lime leaves, and onion after simmering. Bring the broth back to a simmer. **(5)** Add shrimp to stock and simmer until pink and opaque, 3–5 minutes. Add fish sauce and salt. **(6)** Place cooked noodles in four bowls. Add hot shrimp soup to the noodles. Pour lime juice over each dish. **(7)** Add fresh cilantro, bean sprouts, thinly sliced red Chile, and lime wedges.

LEMONGRASS-GALANGAL SHRIMP PHO

Preparation Time: 30 minutes || Cooking Time: 1 hour || Servings: 4 servings

Ingredients:

1 tablespoon vegetable oil	2 stalks lemongrass, tender parts only, finely chopped
2 inches galangal, thinly sliced	1 large onion, halved and thinly sliced
2 cloves garlic, minced	6 cups chicken or vegetable broth
1-pound large shrimp, peeled and deveined	200 grams of rice noodles
2 tablespoons fish sauce	Salt, to taste
1 lime, juiced	Fresh cilantro for garnish
Bean sprouts, for garnish	Thinly sliced green chili for garnish
Lime wedges for serving	

Instructions:

(1) Heat vegetable oil in a big saucepan on medium. Combine lemongrass, galangal, onion, and garlic. Stir regularly until onions are tender, approximately 5 minutes. **(2)** Boil the water in the pot. To add more taste, turn down the heat and let it cook for 30 minutes. **(3)** Prepare the rice noodles per the box while the broth simmers; set aside. **(4)** Strain the broth to remove lemongrass, galangal, and any solids after cooking. Return the clear broth to the pot and boil. **(5)** The shrimp should be pink and cooked in 3–5 minutes in the boiling liquid. Add fish sauce and salt to taste. **(6)** To serve, split noodles among four bowls. Heat shrimp soup and pour over noodles. Squeeze lime juice into each bowl. **(7)** Add cilantro, bean sprouts, and thinly sliced green Chile. Accompany with lime wedges and serve immediately.

LAI CHAU STYLE BEEF PHO

Preparation Time: 30 minutes || Cooking Time: 2 hours || Servings: 4

Ingredients:

1 lb (450g) beef brisket, thinly sliced	8 cups (2 liters) beef broth
2 onions, sliced	4 cloves garlic, minced
2-inch piece ginger, sliced	2-star anise
3 whole cloves	1 cinnamon stick
2 tablespoons fish sauce	1 tablespoon sugar
Salt, to taste	Rice noodles, cooked according to package instructions
Fresh herbs (cilantro, Thai basil, mint)	Bean sprouts
Lime wedges	Chili peppers, thinly sliced

Instructions:

(1) Beef broth, onions, garlic, ginger, star anise, cloves, cinnamon stick, fish sauce, and sugar should all be combined in a big saucepan. **(2)** When it starts to boil, turn down the heat and let it cook for an hour. **(3)** When the meat is cooked, add the sliced beef brisket to the stock and simmer for an additional hour. **(4)** Add salt to taste to season. **(5)** As you wait, prepare the rice noodles per the directions on the box. After draining, set away. **(6)** Spoon the cooked noodles into dishes to serve. Over the noodles, ladle the boiling soup and steak. **(7)** Add sliced Chile peppers, bean sprouts, lime wedges, and fresh herbs as garnish. **(8)** Enjoy while hot!

DIEN BIEN STYLE BEEF PHO

Preparation Time: 20 minutes || Cooking Time: 2 hours || Servings: 4

Ingredients:

1 lb (450g) beef sirloin, thinly sliced	8 cups (2 liters) beef broth

2 onions, chopped
2-inch piece ginger, grated
1 tablespoon fennel seeds
1 tablespoon sugar
Rice noodles
Scallions, thinly sliced
Lime wedges
Sriracha sauce
4 cloves garlic, minced
1 tablespoon coriander seeds
2 tablespoons fish sauce
Salt, to taste
Fresh cilantro, chopped
Thai basil leaves
Hoisin sauce

Instructions:

(1) Beef broth, fish sauce, sugar, coriander, fennel, and onion seeds should all be combined in a big saucepan. **(2)** When it starts to boil, turn down the heat and let it cook for an hour. **(3)** After adding the sliced beef sirloin to the stock, boil it for an additional hour or until the meat is well-cooked. **(4)** Add salt to taste to season. **(5)** As you wait, prepare the rice noodles per the directions on the box. After draining, set away. **(6)** Spoon the cooked noodles into dishes to serve. Over the noodles, ladle the boiling soup and steak. **(7)** Add lime wedges, Thai basil leaves, sliced scallions, and chopped cilantro as garnish. **(8)** To add more kick to the pho or to dip it in, serve it with hoisin and sriracha sauce on the side. **(9)** Savor the flavor of your Dine Bien Style Beef Pho!

LANG SON STYLE BEEF PHO

Preparation Time: 25 minutes || Cooking Time: 2 hours 30 minutes || Servings: 4

Ingredients:

1 lb (450g) beef flank, thinly sliced
2 onions, thinly sliced
2-inch piece ginger, sliced
1 tablespoon whole black peppercorns
1 tablespoon sugar
Rice noodles
Bean sprouts
Sliced jalapeños
8 cups (2 liters) beef broth
4 cloves garlic, minced
1 tablespoon whole coriander seeds
2 tablespoons fish sauce
Salt, to taste
Fresh Thai basil leaves
Lime wedges
Hoisin sauce
Sriracha sauce

Instructions:

(1) Beef broth, onions, garlic, ginger, coriander seeds, black peppercorns, fish sauce, and sugar should all be combined in a big saucepan. **(2)** When it starts to boil, turn down the heat and let it cook for an hour. **(3)** When the beef is cooked, add the sliced flank to the stock and simmer for an additional hour. **(4)** Add salt to taste to season. **(5)** As you wait, prepare the rice noodles per the directions on the box. After draining, set away. **(6)** Spoon the cooked noodles into dishes to serve. Over the noodles, ladle the boiling soup and steak. **(7)** Add sliced jalapeños, bean sprouts, lime wedges, and fresh Thai basil leaves as garnish. **(8)** Serve alongside hoisin and sriracha sauces for dipping or extra flavor. **(9)** Savor the delicious and fragrant Lang Son Style Beef Pho!

THAI NGUYEN STYLE BEEF PHO

Preparation Time: 20 minutes || Cooking Time: 8 hours (for broth), 30 minutes (assembly) || Servings: 4-6

Ingredients:

2 lbs beef bones (with marrow)
2 onions, charred
2-star anise
4 cloves
1 tsp fennel seeds
6 liters water
Salt, to taste
200g beef sirloin, thinly sliced
1 bunch cilantro, chopped
1 lb beef brisket
4-inch piece of ginger, charred
2 cinnamon sticks
1 tsp coriander seeds
1 cardamom pod
2 tbsp fish sauce
400g rice noodles, cooked
1 bunch green onions, sliced
Bean sprouts, lime wedges, basil, and sliced chili for serving

Instructions:

(1) Bathe beef bones in cold water. Put brisket in a big saucepan with 6 liters of water and boil. Remove surface scum. **(2)** Add charred onions, ginger, star anise, cinnamon sticks, cloves, coriander seeds, fennel seeds, and cardamom pod. Simmer partially covered for 8 hours on low heat. Make sure bones are immersed with water. **(3)** Remove and save brisket. Sieve the broth finely. Add fish sauce and salt to taste. **(4)** Pho assembly: Place cooked noodles in bowls. Thinly slice cooked brisket. Top noodles with brisket pieces, raw sirloin (it cooks in hot soup), green onions, and cilantro. **(5)** Cover dishes with hot broth. Quickly serve with bean sprouts, lime wedges, basil, and chopped chiles.

HA NAM STYLE BEEF PHO

Preparation Time: 30 minutes || Cooking Time: 6 hours (for broth), 30 minutes (assembly) || Servings: 4-6

Ingredients:

2 lbs beef bones	1 lb beef oxtail
2 onions, charred	4-inch piece of ginger, charred
1 cinnamon stick	3-star anise
1 tsp black peppercorns	6 liters water
2 tbsp fish sauce	Salt, to taste
400g rice noodles, cooked	200g beef sirloin, thinly sliced
Green onions, sliced, for garnish	Cilantro, for garnish
Lime wedges, hoisin sauce, and sriracha for serving	

Instructions:

(1) Put the oxtail and beef bones into a big saucepan, add water to cover, and heat until it boils. Remove dirt with a skim. Add the peppercorns, star anise, cinnamon, ginger, and burnt onions after lowering the heat. Simmer for six hours. **(2)** Remove the oxtail and bones; drain the soup. Add salt and fish sauce for seasoning. **(3)** Assemble bowls with raw sirloin pieces, cooked noodles, and cilantro and green onions as garnish. **(4)** Fill each dish with heated broth. Accompany with lime wedges, sriracha, and hoisin sauce.

NAM DINH STYLE BEEF PHO

Preparation Time: 25 minutes || Cooking Time: 7 hours (for broth), 20 minutes (assembly) || Servings: 4-6

Ingredients:

2 lbs beef marrow bones	1 lb beef flank
1 large onion, charred	4-inch piece of ginger, charred
5-star anise	3 cloves
1 cinnamon stick	1 tsp cardamom seeds
6 liters water	2 tbsp fish sauce
Salt, to taste	400g rice noodles, cooked
200g beef tenderloin, thinly sliced	Fresh herbs (cilantro, basil) for garnish
Bean sprouts, lime wedges, and sliced chili for serving	

Instructions:

(1) In a big saucepan, boil the flank and bones of beef. Remove dirt with a skim. Add the cardamom seeds, cloves, cinnamon, star anise, ginger, and charred onion. Simmer for seven hours. **(2)** Take out the meat and drain the broth. Tear the side apart. Add salt and fish sauce to flavor the soup. **(3)** Place noodles in dishes and garnish with raw tenderloin pieces, shredded flank, and herbs. **(4)** Top with heated broth and garnish with Chile, lime wedges, and bean sprouts.

THANH HOA STYLE BEEF PHO

Preparation Time: 30 minutes || Cooking Time: 2 hours || Servings: 4

Ingredients:

2 lbs beef bones	1 lb beef brisket
1 large onion, halved and unpeeled	4-inch piece of ginger, halved lengthwise
2 cinnamon sticks	3-star anise
3 cloves	1 teaspoon coriander seeds
1 tablespoon salt	4 tablespoons fish sauce

2 tablespoons sugar
Rice noodles (pho), as needed

Hoisin sauce and chili sauce for serving

8 cups water
Fresh herbs (cilantro, basil), thinly sliced onions, green onions, and lime wedges for garnish

Instructions:

(1) Lightly blacken onion and ginger under the broiler or burner. Wash. **(2)** Place beef bones and brisket in a large saucepan. Add cold water and boil. For 10 minutes, boil hard. Rinse bones with warm water. Replace the bones and brisket in the pot. **(3)** The saucepan should contain 8 cups of water, charred onion, ginger, cinnamon sticks, star anise, cloves, coriander seeds, salt, fish sauce, and sugar. First, boil, then gently simmer for 1.5 to 2 hours to tenderize beef brisket. **(4)** Let the brisket cool. Slice brisket thinly. **(5)** Strain and return broth to pot. Over medium heat, season soup with salt and fish sauce. **(6)** Make rice noodles as directed. **(7)** Dish noodles into bowls. Top with brisket. Top with hot broth. Decorate with fresh herbs, green onions, and lime wedges. Add hoisin and chili sauces.

NGHE AN STYLE BEEF PHO

Preparation Time: 30 minutes || Cooking Time: 2 hours 30 minutes || Servings: 4

Ingredients:

2 lbs beef marrow bones
1 large onion, halved and unpeeled
2 black cardamom pods
2 cinnamon sticks
4 tablespoons fish sauce
8 cups water
Fresh herbs (cilantro, mint), bean sprouts, thinly sliced onions, and lime wedges for garnish

1 lb beef shank
1 4-inch piece of ginger, halved lengthwise
4-star anise
1 tablespoon salt
1 tablespoon sugar
Rice noodles (pho), as needed
Hoisin sauce and Sriracha for serving

Instructions:

(1) Char onion and ginger till slightly browned under the broiler or open flame. Cleanly rinse. **(2)** Add beef bones and shank to a large saucepan. Cover with cold water and boil. Drain and rinse bones and saucepan after 10 minutes of boiling. **(3)** Put the cleaned bones, shank, 8 cups of water, charred onion, ginger, black cardamom, star anise, cinnamon sticks, salt, fish sauce, and sugar back in the saucepan. After boiling, simmer for 2–2.5 hours to tenderize the meat. **(4)** After cooling, slice the beef shank thinly. **(5)** Return the strained broth to the pot. Heat and season broth. **(6)** Prepare the rice noodles per the packet. **(7)** Put noodles in dishes, add beef shank pieces, and pour heated broth over. Add herbs, bean sprouts, onions, and lime wedges. Accompany with hoisin and Sriracha.

HA TINH STYLE BEEF PHO

Preparation Time: 40 minutes || Cooking Time: 2 hours || Servings: 4

Ingredients:

2 lbs beef knuckle bones
1 large onion, halved and unpeeled
5-star anise
1 teaspoon black peppercorns
4 tablespoons fish sauce
8 cups water
Fresh herbs (cilantro, green onions), bean sprouts, thinly sliced onions, and lime wedges for garnish

1 lb beef round
1 4-inch piece of ginger, halved lengthwise
3 cinnamon sticks
1 tablespoon salt
1 tablespoon sugar
Rice noodles (pho), as needed
Chili paste and lime juice for serving

Instructions:

(1) Char onion and ginger till slightly browned under the broiler or open flame. Cleanly rinse. **(2)** Add beef bones and cold water to a big saucepan. Boil vigorously for 10 minutes. Remove bones and flesh, drain, and clean the pot. **(3)** Return bones, meat, 8 cups water, charred onion, ginger, star anise, cinnamon sticks, black peppercorns, salt, fish sauce, and sugar to the pot. Simmer for 2 hours after boiling to tenderize meat. **(4)** Cut the beef round thinly after cooling. **(5)** Return the strained broth to the pot. Adjust seasoning with heat. **(6)** Prepare the rice noodles per the packet. **(7)** Put noodles in dishes, top with beef pieces, then pour heated broth. Add fresh herbs, bean sprouts, onions, and lime wedges. Add chili paste and lime juice for garnish.

QUANG BINH STYLE BEEF PHO

Preparation Time: 30 minutes || Cooking Time: 2 hours || Servings: 4

Ingredients:

1 lb beef brisket	8 cups beef broth
2 cinnamon sticks	4-star anise
4 cloves	2 cardamom pods
1 piece of ginger, sliced	2 onions, quartered
1 tablespoon fish sauce	Salt, to taste
14 oz rice noodles	1 onion, thinly sliced
3 green onions, chopped	Cilantro chopped (for garnish)
Lime wedges for serving	Bean sprouts for serving
Fresh basil leaves for serving	

Instructions:

(1) Cover beef brisket with water in a saucepan. Boil for 10 minutes to eliminate contaminants. Drain and rinse brisket. **(2)** Add beef broth, cinnamon sticks, star anise, cloves, cardamom pods, ginger, quartered onions, and cooked brisket to a clean saucepan. Tenderize the beef by simmering for 1.5 hours after boiling. **(3)** Remove brisket from stew and slice thinly. Return the stock to the pot after straining out spices and onions. Add fish sauce and salt to taste. **(4)** Follow package instructions to cook rice noodles. **(5)** Place rice noodles in each bowl to make pho. Add meat, finely cut onion, and green onions. Cover noodles and meat with heated broth. **(6)** On the side, serve cilantro, lime wedges, bean sprouts, and fresh basil.

QUANG TRI-STYLE BEEF PHO

Preparation Time: 30 minutes || Cooking Time: 2 hours || Servings: 4

Ingredients:

1 lb beef shank	8 cups beef broth
2 lemongrass stalks, crushed	1 cinnamon stick
3-star anise	1 onion, quartered
1 piece of ginger, sliced	1 tablespoon fish sauce
Salt, to taste	14 oz rice noodles
1 onion, thinly sliced	3 green onions, chopped
Cilantro chopped (for garnish)	Lime wedges for serving
Chili slices for serving	

Instructions:

(1) Clean beef shank with a 10-minute boil. Drain, rinse, and set aside. **(2)** Add beef broth, lemongrass, cinnamon stick, star anise, quartered onion, ginger, and cleaned beef shank to a clean saucepan. Boil and then simmer for 2 hours to tenderize the meat. **(3)** Cut the beef shank thinly and lay aside. Remove solids from broth. **(4)** Season broth with fish sauce and salt. **(5)** Prepare rice noodles according to package instructions. **(6)** Place noodles in bowls and top with meat pieces, thinly sliced onion, and green onions. Pour hot broth on top. **(7)** Serve cilantro, lime wedges, and chili slices on the side.

THUA THIEN HUE STYLE BEEF PHO

Preparation Time: 30 minutes || Cooking Time: 2 hours || Servings: 4

Ingredients:

- 1 lb beef bones
- 8 cups water
- 1 piece of ginger, charred
- 1 tablespoon fish sauce
- 14 oz flat rice noodles
- 3 green onions, chopped
- Lime wedges for serving
- Shredded banana blossom for serving (optional)
- 1 lb beef flank
- 2 onions, charred
- 1 lemongrass stalk, crushed
- Salt and sugar, to taste
- 1 onion, thinly sliced
- Cilantro chopped (for garnish)
- Sliced chili for serving

Instructions:

(1) For thirty minutes, roast the beef flank and bones at 400°F in a preheated oven. **(2)** Add water, crushed lemongrass, roasted beef bones, charred ginger, onions, and flank to a large saucepan. After bringing it to a boil, simmer until the meat is cooked for about 2 hours. **(3)** Take off the flank of beef, cut it thinly, and set it aside. Filter the broth to get rid of the solids. **(4)** Add sugar, salt, and fish sauce to season the soup. **(5)** To make flat rice noodles, follow the package instructions. **(6)** To serve, arrange noodles in bowls with thinly sliced onions, green onions, and pieces of meat. Ladle hot broth on top. **(7)** Along with sliced chiles, lime wedges, and shredded banana blossom, garnish with cilantro.

QUANG NAM STYLE BEEF PHO

Preparation Time: 20 minutes || Cooking Time: 3 hours || Servings: 4

Ingredients:

- 1 lb beef bones
- 6 cups beef broth
- 4 cloves garlic, minced
- 2-star anise
- 1 tablespoon fennel seeds
- 2 tablespoons fish sauce
- Rice noodles
- 1 lb beef brisket, thinly sliced
- 2 onions, sliced
- 1 cinnamon stick
- 1 tablespoon coriander seeds
- 1 tablespoon sugar
- Salt, to taste
- Garnishes: bean sprouts, lime wedges, Thai basil, cilantro, sliced chili peppers

Instructions:

(1) Beef bones, brisket, onions, garlic, star anise, cinnamon sticks, coriander seeds, fennel seeds, sugar, fish sauce, and salt should all be added to a big saucepan. **(2)** Cover the contents of the saucepan with the beef broth. Bring over high heat to a boil. **(3)** After a boil, reduce the heat to a simmer for two to three hours, scraping for impurities. **(4)** After taking the brisket out of the cooker, thinly slice it. Put aside. **(5)** Remove the particles from the broth by straining it through a fine-mesh strainer. **(6)** Cook rice noodles according to the box. **(7)** Spoon cooked noodles into dishes to serve. Drizzle some hot broth over the noodles and cover with sliced beef. **(8)** Add bean sprouts, sliced chili peppers, lime wedges, cilantro, and Thai basil as garnish. Warm up the food.

QUANG NGAI STYLE BEEF PHO

Preparation Time: 25 minutes || Cooking Time: 2.5 hours || Servings: 4

Ingredients:

- 1 lb beef bones
- 6 cups beef broth
- 4 cloves garlic, minced
- 2-star anise
- 1 tablespoon fennel seeds
- 2 tablespoons fish sauce
- Rice noodles
- 1 lb beef sirloin, thinly sliced
- 2 onions, sliced
- 1 cinnamon stick
- 1 tablespoon coriander seeds
- 1 tablespoon sugar
- Salt, to taste
- Garnishes: bean sprouts, lime wedges,

Thai basil, cilantro, sliced chili peppers

Instructions:

(1) Beef bones, sirloin, onions, garlic, star anise, cinnamon sticks, coriander seeds, fennel seeds, sugar, fish sauce, and salt should all be combined in a big saucepan. **(2)** Cover the items with the beef broth. Bring over high heat to a boil. **(3)** Lower the temperature to a simmer for around two to three hours, making sure to skim any particles that come to the top. **(4)** After taking the steak out of the pot, thinly slice it. Put aside. **(5)** Remove the particles from the broth by straining it through a fine-mesh strainer. **(6)** Cook rice noodles according to the box. **(7)** Spoon cooked noodles into dishes to serve. Place thinly sliced sirloin on top and pour heated broth over noodles. **(8)** Add bean sprouts, sliced chili peppers, lime wedges, cilantro, and Thai basil as garnish. Warm up the food.

CHAPTER: 7 PHO GARNISHES AND CONDIMENTS:

QUICK-PICKLED FRESH BEAN SPROUTS

Preparation Time: 10 minutes || Cooking Time: 5 minutes || Servings: 4 servings

Ingredients:

2 cups fresh bean sprouts	1 cup water
1 cup vinegar (white or apple cider)	1 tablespoon sugar
1 teaspoon salt	1 small carrot, julienned (optional for added color and flavor)

Instructions:

(1) Thoroughly rinse the bean sprouts with cool water. After draining, set away. **(2)** Place water, vinegar, sugar, and salt in a pot. Salt and sugar dissolve in medium heat boiling. **(3)** Take the pot off of the burner. Give the brine five minutes or so to cool. **(4)** Fill a clean jar with the bean sprouts and, if using, the julienned carrot. Make sure the bean sprouts are fully immersed by pouring the warm brine over them. **(5)** Allow the container to reach ambient temperature. After that, seal and chill for a minimum of one hour before serving. You can keep these quickly pickled bean sprouts in the fridge for up to two weeks.

CLASSIC BEEF PHO WITH LIME WEDGES

Preparation Time: 30 minutes || Cooking Time: 6 hours || Servings: 4

Ingredients:

2 lbs beef bones	1 onion, halved and charred
4-inch piece of ginger, halved lengthwise	3-star anise
2 cinnamon sticks	3 cloves
1 cardamom pod	4 quarts water
2 tablespoons fish sauce	1 tablespoon sugar
Salt, to taste	8 oz. rice noodles
1 lb thinly sliced beef sirloin	Fresh cilantro, basil, lime wedges, bean sprouts, hoisin sauce, and Sriracha (for serving)

Instructions:

(1) To create the broth, place the beef bones, onion, ginger, star anise, cinnamon, cloves, and cardamom in a large saucepan and cover with water. Simmer for at least 6 hours. If any foam appears on the surface, skim it off. **(2)** After straining, pour the broth back into the pot. Add salt, sugar, and fish sauce for seasoning. **(3)** Make rice noodles according to the directions on the box. **(4)** Bring the broth to a vigorous boil. When serving dishes, arrange noodles and raw beef pieces. **(5)** Over the noodles and meat, ladle the heated broth. The beef pieces will be cooked by the heat. **(6)** Present the dish alongside fresh herbs, bean sprouts, lime wedges, hoisin sauce, and Sriracha.

CHICKEN PHO WITH SLICED JALAPEÑOS

Preparation Time: 20 minutes || Cooking Time: 1 hour || Servings: 4

Ingredients:

1 large chicken breast	1 onion, halved and charred
4-inch piece of ginger, halved lengthwise	2-star anise
1 cinnamon stick	4 quarts water
2 tablespoons fish sauce	1 tablespoon sugar
Salt, to taste	8 oz. rice noodles
Sliced jalapeños, cilantro, lime wedges, bean sprouts (for serving)	

Instructions:

(1) Simmer the chicken breast, onion, ginger, star anise, and cinnamon in water for approximately one hour in a big saucepan. **(2)** Shred the chicken after removing it and allowing it to cool. **(3)** After straining, pour the broth back into the pot. Add salt, sugar, and fish sauce for seasoning. **(4)** Make rice noodles according to the directions on the box. **(5)** Transfer the shredded chicken and noodles into serving dishes. **(6)** Over the noodles and chicken, ladle the heated broth. **(7)** Present the dish alongside chopped jalapeños, cilantro, lime wedges, and bean sprouts.

VEGETARIAN PHO WITH THINLY SLICED SCALLIONS

Preparation Time: 20 minutes || Cooking Time: 45 minutes || Servings: 4

Ingredients:

4 quarts vegetable broth	1 onion, halved and charred
4-inch piece of ginger, halved lengthwise	2-star anise
1 cinnamon stick	2 tablespoons soy sauce
1 tablespoon sugar	Salt, to taste
8 oz. rice noodles	1 cup sliced mushrooms
1 cup Bok choy, chopped	Thinly sliced scallions, cilantro, lime wedges, bean sprouts (for serving)

Instructions:

(1) Simmer the onion, ginger, star anise, and cinnamon in a large saucepan with vegetable stock for around 45 minutes. **(2)** After straining, pour the broth back into the pot. Add salt, sugar, and soy sauce for seasoning. **(3)** Make rice noodles according to the directions on the box. **(4)** Bok choy and mushrooms should be sautéed till soft. **(5)** When serving dishes, combine noodles and sautéed veggies. **(6)** Over the noodles and veggies, ladle the heated broth. **(7)** Serve with bean sprouts, lime wedges, cilantro, and thinly sliced scallions on the side.

QUICK-PICKLED BEAN SPROUTS

Preparation Time: 10 minutes || Cooking Time: 5 minutes || Servings: 4 servings

Ingredients:

2 cups fresh bean sprouts	1 cup water
1/2 cup vinegar (white or rice vinegar)	2 tablespoons sugar
1 teaspoon salt	

Instructions:

(1) After giving the bean sprouts a good rinse in cold water, drain them. **(2)** Utilize a pot to mix vinegar, sugar, salt, water, and more. Stir in sugar and salt over medium heat to boil. **(3)** Transfer the bean sprouts to a heat-resistant dish. Make sure the bean sprouts are completely soaked by pouring the hot pickling liquid over them. **(4)** Cool the mixture to room temp. Serve after one hour of refrigeration. **(5)** Serve as a tart and crunchy addition to pho or other meals.

CLASSIC LIME BEEF PHO

Preparation Time: 30 minutes || Cooking Time: 6 hours || Servings: 4

Ingredients:

- 2 onions, halved and unpeeled
- 3 pounds beef bones (mix of marrow and knuckle bones)
- 3-star anise
- 1 cardamom pod
- 4 tablespoons fish sauce
- 1 pound beef sirloin, thinly sliced
- 1 lime, cut into wedges
- Bean sprouts, lime wedges, hoisin sauce, and Sriracha (for serving)
- 1 4-inch piece of ginger, halved lengthwise
- 1 cinnamon stick
- 3 cloves
- 1 tablespoon salt
- 2 tablespoons sugar
- 8 ounces rice noodles
- Fresh herbs (cilantro, basil)

Instructions:

(1) Heat the oven to 425°F. Roast onions and ginger on a baking sheet for 30 minutes until slightly browned. **(2)** Boil 4 quarts of water in a big saucepan. Add beef bones and boil hard for 10 minutes. Strain and wash bones with warm water. Clear the pot and return the bones. **(3)** Add 4 quarts of fresh water, bones, charred onions, ginger, cinnamon, star anise, cloves, cardamom, salt, fish sauce, and sugar to the saucepan. Heat to boiling, then simmer. Cover and simmer for 6+ hours. **(4)** Return the strained broth to the pot. Salt, fish sauce, and sugar can be added as needed. **(5)** Follow package instructions to cook rice noodles. Divide noodles into bowls. **(6)** Place steak sirloin pieces on noodles. Pour heated broth on meat to cook. Serve alongside lime wedges, fresh herbs, bean sprouts, hoisin sauce, and Sriracha.

SPICY JALAPEÑO CHICKEN PHO

Preparation Time: 20 minutes || Cooking Time: 1 hour || Servings: 4

Ingredients:

- 1 large onion, quartered
- 2 pounds of chicken bones or carcass
- 1 cinnamon stick
- 4 cloves
- 3 tablespoons fish sauce
- 1 pound chicken breast, thinly sliced
- Fresh cilantro and sliced jalapeños for garnish
- 1 4-inch piece of ginger, halved lengthwise
- 2 jalapeños, sliced (adjust to taste)
- 2-star anise
- 1 tablespoon salt
- 1 tablespoon sugar
- 8 ounces rice noodles
- Bean sprouts, lime wedges, and hoisin sauce (for serving)

Instructions:

(1) Add the onion and ginger to a large saucepan and roast over medium heat until just starting to turn black, about 5 minutes. **(2)** Stir in 4 quarts of water, jalapeños, cinnamon, star anise, cloves, fish sauce, sugar, and chicken bones. After it boils, turn down the heat and let it cook for an hour. **(3)** After straining, pour the broth back into the pot. If necessary, adjust the seasoning with more salt, sugar, or fish sauce. **(4)** To make rice noodles, follow the package instructions. In bowls, place noodles. **(5)** Place chicken breast pieces on top of the noodles. To cook the chicken, pour boiling broth over it. Add sliced jalapeños and cilantro as garnish. Present the dish alongside bean sprouts, lime wedges, and hoisin sauce.

SCALLION GINGER BEEF PHO

Preparation Time: 30 minutes || Cooking Time: 6 hours || Servings: 4

Ingredients:

- 2 onions, halved
- 3 pounds of beef bones
- 1 cinnamon stick
- 2 cloves
- 4 tablespoons fish sauce
- 1 pound beef sirloin, thinly sliced
- 1 4-inch piece of ginger, sliced
- 1 bunch scallions, chopped
- 3-star anise
- 1 tablespoon salt
- 2 tablespoons sugar
- 8 ounces rice noodles

Scallions and fresh herbs for garnish	Bean sprouts, lime wedges, hoisin sauce, and Sriracha (for serving)

Instructions:

(1) In a dry skillet over medium heat, caramelize onions and ginger until gently browned. **(2)** Boil the beef bones in water for ten minutes in a big saucepan. After draining and rinsing, add the bones back to the saucepan along with sugar, salt, fish sauce, cloves, charred onions, ginger, scallions, cinnamon, and star anise. Simmer for six hours. **(3)** Keep the soup heated, strain it, and adjust the spice. **(4)** Make rice noodles according to the directions on the box. Distribute among bowls. **(5)** Place beef pieces over the noodles. To cook the steak, pour heated broth over the top. Add fresh herbs and scallions as garnish. Accompany with sides.

FRIED SHALLOTS

Preparation Time: 5 minutes || Cooking Time: 10 minutes || Servings: 4 servings

Ingredients:

300g shallots, thinly sliced	500ml vegetable oil, for frying
A pinch of salt	

Instructions:

(1) Thinly slice the shallots after peeling them. To ensure consistent cooking, make sure they are of the same thickness. **(2)** Use a medium-sized frying pan to heat vegetable oil. To test oil readiness, drop a shallot into it; it should sizzle. **(3)** Add the cut shallots to the oil very carefully. To make sure they don't stay together, gently stir. **(4)** Shallots should be fried until crispy and golden brown, stirring from time to time. This ought to take ten to fifteen minutes. **(5)** Spoon the shallots out of the oil and place them on a paper towel-lined plate. Salt on top. **(6)** Let the shallots cool fully in the oil. They can be kept for up to a week in an airtight container or used right away.

THAI CHILI PEPPERS (CHILI OIL)

Preparation Time: 10 minutes || Cooking Time: 5 minutes || Servings: About 1 cup

Ingredients:

1 cup vegetable oil	2 tablespoons sesame oil
1/2 cup dried Thai chili peppers, crushed	3 cloves garlic, minced
1 teaspoon salt	1 tablespoon soy sauce

Instructions:

(1) Sesame and vegetable oils should be heated but not smoked in a small pot over low heat. **(2)** Crush the Thai chili peppers and add them to the oil. Mix it all together slowly. **(3)** Make sure not to let the mixture burn by cooking it on low heat for around 5 minutes. Fragrance should be present in the oil. **(4)** Take off the heat and mix in the soy sauce and salt. Allow the hot sauce to come down to room temperature. **(5)** After the Chile oil cools, pour it into a container or jar. You may use the Chile oil right away or keep it in the fridge for up to a month.

HOISIN SAUCE

Preparation Time: 5 minutes || Cooking Time: 10 minutes || Servings: About 1 cup

Ingredients:

4 tablespoons soy sauce	2 tablespoons peanut butter or a nut-free alternative
1 tablespoon honey or molasses	2 teaspoons white vinegar
1/8 teaspoon garlic powder	2 teaspoons sesame oil
20 drops hot sauce, adjust to taste	1/8 teaspoon black pepper

Instructions:

(1) A small bowl is used to mix the peanut butter and soy sauce together until they are well mixed. **(2)** Incorporate the white vinegar, honey, black pepper, sesame oil, spicy sauce, and garlic powder. Mixing all the components thoroughly requires whisking. **(3)** On low heat, stir the mixture in a small saucepan until thick and shiny. Take 10–15 minutes. **(4)** Take off the heat source and let the hoisin sauce reach room temperature. **(5)** The hoisin sauce can be used right away after cooling or kept in the fridge for up to two weeks if kept in an airtight container.

HOMEMADE SRIRACHA SAUCE

Preparation Time: 15 minutes || Cooking Time: 20 minutes || Servings: Makes about 2 cups

Ingredients:

1-pound red jalapeño peppers, stemmed and sliced	4 garlic cloves
3 tablespoons light brown sugar	1 tablespoon kosher salt
1/2 cup distilled white vinegar	2 tablespoons water

Instructions:

(1) In a food processor, combine the jalapeños, garlic, brown sugar, and salt. Pulse until chopped finely. **(2)** Once the mixture is in a clean jar, cover it and let it sit for three to five days at room temperature, stirring once a day. The mixture will start to boil and ferment. **(3)** Once the mixture has finished fermenting, pour it into a saucepan, add the vinegar and water, and heat until it boils. After lowering the heat, simmer for five to ten minutes. **(4)** After allowing the liquid to cool somewhat, combine it until it's smooth. **(5)** Press to extract as much liquid as possible from the sauce while you strain it through a fine-mesh screen to remove the pulp. **(6)** Refrigerate the Sriracha sauce after transferring it to a fresh bottle or jar. For optimal flavor, use within six months.

HOMEMADE FISH SAUCE

Preparation Time: 10 minutes (plus 6 months fermentation) || Cooking Time: 0 minutes || Servings: Makes about 2 cups

Ingredients:

1 pound fresh, small whole fish (anchovies, sardines), cleaned	1/3 cup sea salt
2 cups water	

Instructions:

(1) Fish and salt should be layered in a clean container, with salt at the top and bottom. **(2)** Water should be added gradually until the fish are fully submerged. **(3)** For around six months, store the jar in a cold, dark area and seal it firmly. Make sure the fish are immersed by checking from time to time and adding extra salty water if needed. **(4)** After the fermentation process, strain the liquid once more through cheesecloth and a fine mesh screen to eliminate any remaining particles. **(5)** Pour the fish sauce into a sanitized bottle. Within a year, it can be utilized after being kept at room temperature.

HOMEMADE SOY SAUCE

Preparation Time: 15 minutes (plus 6 months fermentation) || Cooking Time: 3 hours || Servings: Makes about 2 cups

Ingredients:

1 cup soybeans	2 cups wheat flour
2 cups water	1 cup sea salt
Aspergillus oryzae (koji) mold spores	

Instructions:

(1) Soak the soybeans for the whole night and boil until tender. Make a paste out of them. **(2)** Stir the wheat flour into the mashed soybeans after pan-roasting it till golden brown. **(3)** Spread the mixture out on a tray, add the koji mold spores, and let it ferment for three days in a warm, humid environment. **(4)** Roughly chop the moldy soybean and wheat combination, then combine it with brine (sea salt and water). Place in a jar, seal, and allow to ferment for six months, stirring now and again. **(5)** After the mixture has fermented, strain it through a cloth to collect the liquid. You can use this soy sauce.

(6) After about 30 minutes of boiling to pasteurize the collected liquid, let it cool. **(7)** Place in a cold, dark location after transferring to a clean bottle. Use in a year or two.

OYSTER SAUCE

Preparation Time: 10 minutes || Cooking Time: 10 minutes || Servings: Makes about 1 cup

Ingredients:

1/2 cup oyster juice (from fresh oysters or canned)	1 tablespoon soy sauce
1 tablespoon light brown sugar	1 tablespoon cornstarch
2 teaspoons water	1/2 teaspoon fish sauce (optional)
Salt, to taste	

Instructions:

(1) Mix the light brown sugar, soy sauce, and oyster juice together in a small pot. Stirring periodically, cook over medium heat until the sugar melts. **(2)** To make a slurry, combine the cornstarch and two tablespoons of water in a small bowl. **(3)** Add the cornstarch slurry to the saucepan when the oyster juice mixture has warmed through, and the sugar has completely dissolved. For two to three minutes, or until the sauce thickens, stir constantly. **(4)** Add the fish sauce, if using, and taste. If needed, adjust the flavor by adding a little salt. **(5)** Put the food away and let it cool down. Cooling makes the sauce thicker. Keep in the fridge for two weeks in a jar that won't let air in.

CHILI GARLIC SAUCE

Preparation Time: 15 minutes || Cooking Time: 20 minutes || Servings: Makes about 1 cup

Ingredients:

1/2 cup fresh red chili peppers, stemmed and chopped	8 cloves garlic, minced
1/4 cup distilled white vinegar	1/4 cup water
2 tablespoons sugar	1 teaspoon salt

Instructions:

(1) Blend or process the garlic, vinegar, water, and chili peppers together in a blender or food processor. Process until it's smooth. **(2)** Pour the mixture into a saucepan and season with salt and sugar. Bring the mixture to a boil while cooking over medium heat, stirring from time to time. **(3)** Simmer the sauce for fifteen minutes, or until it slightly thickens, on low heat. **(4)** Do not heat it anymore. Let it cool down. However, it will get thicker as it cools. **(5)** Refrigerate after transferring to an airtight container. Store the sauce in the refrigerator for up to one month.

PICKLED GARLIC

Preparation Time: 15 minutes (plus 2 weeks for pickling) || Cooking Time: 5 minutes || Servings: Makes about 1 cup

Ingredients:

1 cup garlic cloves, peeled	1 cup distilled white vinegar
1 cup water	1 tablespoon sugar
1 teaspoon salt	1 teaspoon black peppercorns
1 bay leaf	

Instructions:

(1) For one minute, blanch the garlic cloves in boiling water. After draining, move to a glass jar. **(2)** Mix the vinegar, sugar, salt, peppercorns, bay leaf, and water in a saucepan. After bringing to a boil, turn off the heat. **(3)** Make sure the garlic cloves in the container are completely soaked by pouring the hot vinegar mixture over them. **(4)** Once the jar has reached room temperature, seal it and place it in the fridge. Before using, let the garlic pickle for at least two weeks. **(5)** You may keep the pickled garlic in the refrigerator for up to three months.

PICKLED JALAPEÑOS

Preparation Time: 10 minutes || Cooking Time: 5 minutes || Servings: Makes about 2 cups

Ingredients:

1 cup water	1 cup white vinegar
2 tablespoons sugar	1 tablespoon kosher salt
2 cloves garlic, peeled and slightly crushed	1 teaspoon oregano (optional for added flavor)
10-12 fresh jalapeños, sliced into rings	

Instructions:

(1) Small pot with water, vinegar, sugar, and salt. Mix the sugar and salt into the juice while heating it over medium-low heat. **(2)** Take the pot off the heat and add the garlic and herbs to the mix. **(3)** Transfer the chopped jalapeños into a sanitized, airtight container. Make sure the jalapeños are completely soaked by pouring the hot vinegar mixture over them. If needed, push the jalapeños down with a spoon. **(4)** Wait until the mixture is at room temperature. Seal the jar after cooling. **(5)** Before serving, place the pickled jalapeños in the refrigerator for a minimum of 24 hours to let the flavors combine. You may keep them in the fridge for up to two months.

PICKLED CARROTS

Preparation Time: 15 minutes || Cooking Time: 5 minutes || Servings: Makes about 2 cups

Ingredients:

1 cup water	1 cup distilled white vinegar
1/4 cup sugar	2 tablespoons kosher salt
4-5 medium carrots, peeled and cut into batons	2 cloves of garlic, peeled
1 teaspoon mustard seeds	

Instructions:

(1) Cook water, vinegar, sugar, and salt in a saucepan on medium. Stir to dissolve sugar and salt while boiling. **(2)** Include mustard seeds and garlic in the boiling mixture. **(3)** Take a clean, heatproof jar and put the carrot batons in it. Make sure the carrots are well-soaked before pouring the hot vinegar mixture over them. If necessary, push down on the carrots with a spoon. **(4)** Cover the jar when the mixture cools to room temperature. **(5)** Refrigerate 24 hours before serving to blend flavors. Limit one month in the fridge.

PICKLED DAIKON RADISH

Preparation Time: 15 minutes || Cooking Time: 5 minutes || Servings: Makes about 2 cups

Ingredients:

1 cup water	1 cup rice vinegar
1/2 cup sugar	2 tablespoons kosher salt
1 pound daikon radish, peeled and cut into thin rounds or matchsticks	2 cloves garlic, peeled
1/2 teaspoon black peppercorns	

Instructions:

(1) Pour water, rice vinegar, sugar, and salt into a saucepan. Over medium heat, melt salt and sugar. Heat to simmer. **(2)** Include the black peppercorns and garlic in the vinegar mixture. **(3)** Transfer the matchsticks or daikon radish slices to a sterile, airtight container. Cover the daikon completely with the hot vinegar mixture after pouring it over it. If needed, push down the daikon with a spoon. **(4)** Replace the jar cover firmly once the mixture cools to room temperature. **(5)** To let the flavors meld, place the pickled daikon in the refrigerator for at least 24 hours. You may store these pickles in the fridge for up to a month.

SLICED RED CHILIES

Preparation Time: 10 minutes || Cooking Time: N/A || Servings: Makes about 1/2 cup

Ingredients:

1/2 cup fresh red	1/4 cup rice vinegar

chilies, thinly sliced
1 tablespoon sugar   1/2 teaspoon salt

Instructions:

(1) Mix sugar, salt, and rice vinegar in a small bowl. Dissolve salt and sugar by mixing. **(2)** Cut the red chilies thinly. You can take out the seeds if you'd rather have less heat. **(3)** Sliced chiles should be added to the vinegar mixture. Before serving, let it rest for at least an hour. This lets the flavors mingle, and the chiles pickle a little. **(4)** Add to pho or other Vietnamese dishes. Refrigerate leftovers in an airtight container.

CRUSHED PEANUTS

Preparation Time: 5 minutes || Cooking Time: 5 minutes || Servings: Makes about 1 cup

Ingredients:

1 cup raw peanuts (without the skin)

Instructions:

(1) Heat a dry skillet to medium. The skillet should have one layer of raw peanuts. **(2)** Toast the peanuts for approximately 5 minutes, stirring regularly, or until aromatic and golden. Take caution not to scorch them. **(3)** After taking the peanuts out of the skillet, let them cool for a little while. **(4)** After cooling, coarsely crush the peanuts in a mortar and pestle or food processor. Textures from microscopic pieces to finely ground are desired. **(5)** To add crunch and taste to salads, pho, and other foods, use it as a topping. Any leftovers should be kept in an airtight container.

FRIED GARLIC

Preparation Time: 5 minutes || Cooking Time: 10 minutes || Servings: Makes about 1/4 cup

Ingredients:

1/2 cup garlic cloves, thinly sliced   1/2 cup vegetable oil

Instructions:

(1) Peel and finely slice garlic. Make consistent slices for even cooking. **(2)** Cook vegetable oil in a small pot on medium. Stir garlic into the oil. **(3)** Stir often and watch the garlic cook. Cook garlic slices till golden. The procedure should take 8-10 minutes. **(4)** Remove cooked garlic slices from oil with a slotted spoon and drain on paper towels. **(5)** Fried garlic adds flavor to pho, soups, and salads after cooling. Garlic-flavored residual oil can be used in dressings or cooking. **(6)** Keep fried garlic in an airtight container at room temperature.

CHILI OIL

Preparation Time: 10 minutes || Cooking Time: 10 minutes || Servings: Approximately 1 cup

Ingredients:

1 cup neutral oil (vegetable or canola oil)	3 tablespoons crushed red pepper flakes
2 teaspoons Szechuan peppercorns	2-star anise
3 cloves garlic, smashed	1-inch piece of ginger, sliced
1 cinnamon stick	1 tablespoon soy sauce (optional)

Instructions:

(1) Oil should be heated in a small saucepan over medium heat. **(2)** Heat oil and add crushed red pepper flakes, Szechuan peppercorns, star anise, garlic, ginger, and cinnamon stick. **(3)** Stir often for 8–10 minutes until the oil smells and the ingredients crackle. **(4)** Turn off the heat and let the oil cool. **(5)** After cooling, filter the oil into a clean, sealed jar using a fine-mesh sieve or cheesecloth. **(6)** Discard or reuse solids. **(7)** Chili oil can be refrigerated for a month.

SESAME OIL

Preparation Time: 5 minutes || Cooking Time: 10 minutes || Servings: Approximately 1 cup

Ingredients:

1 cup sesame seeds   2 cups neutral oil

(vegetable or canola oil)

Instructions:

(1) A dry pan over medium heat should toast sesame seeds for 5-7 minutes, turning occasionally, until golden brown and fragrant. **(2)** Remove roasted sesame seeds from the pan and cool fully. **(3)** Mix sesame seeds in a blender or food processor after cooling. **(4)** Blend sesame seeds into a coarse pulp. **(5)** Heat neutral oil in a small pot on medium until 350°F (175°C). **(6)** In the blender or food processor, carefully pour heated oil over sesame paste. **(7)** Blend until smooth and properly mixed. **(8)** Cool the sesame oil before putting it in a clean, airtight container. **(9)** Store sesame oil in a dark, cool area for six months.

RICE VINEGAR

Preparation Time: 5 minutes || Cooking Time: 15 minutes || Servings: Approximately 1 cup

Ingredients:

- 2 cups unseasoned rice vinegar
- 1/2 teaspoon salt
- 1/4 cup granulated sugar

Instructions:

(1) Add the salt, granulated sugar, and rice vinegar to a small pot. **(2)** Simmer and whisk the liquid over medium heat until the sugar and salt dissolve. **(3)** After the ingredients dissolve, remove the pot from the heat and let the liquid cool. **(4)** After cooling down, pour the rice vinegar into a fresh, sealed bottle or jar. **(5)** The rice vinegar may be kept in the refrigerator for up to six months.

HOMEMADE MIRIN

Preparation Time: 5 minutes || Cooking Time: 30 minutes || Servings: Makes about 2 cups

Ingredients:

- 1 cup's sake (Japanese rice wine)
- 2 tablespoons glutinous rice or sweet rice (optional for added body and sweetness)
- 1 cup granulated sugar

Instructions:

(1) Heat a saucepan with the sake and sugar mixture over medium heat. Add the glutinous rice right away if using it. **(2)** Mix the blend until all the sugar has dissolved. **(3)** After the sugar has completely dissolved, turn down the heat to low and simmer the liquid for about half an hour. The mixture ought to somewhat thicken and get syrupy. **(4)** Take it off the stove and let it come to room temperature. Strain out any sticky rice that you may have used. **(5)** Transfer the mirin into a sterile, clean bottle. Keep firmly sealed and keep in a dark, cool location. Over time, the flavor of the mirin will continue to develop and soften.

BROWN SUGAR BEEF PHO

Preparation Time: 20 minutes || Cooking Time: 6 hours (slow cooking for broth) || Servings: 4-6

Ingredients:

- 1.5 lbs beef bones
- 4 cloves garlic, charred
- 3-star anise
- 4 cardamom pods
- 8 cups water
- Salt, to taste
- 1 lb beef sirloin, thinly sliced
- 1 onion, halved and charred
- 2-inch ginger, charred
- 2 cinnamon sticks
- 1/4 cup brown sugar
- 2 tablespoons fish sauce
- 200g rice noodles
- Fresh herbs (cilantro, basil, mint), bean sprouts, lime wedges, and sliced chili for garnish

Instructions:

(1) Brown sugar, cinnamon, cardamom, star anise, charred onion, garlic, ginger, and meat bones should all be combined in a big saucepan. Add the water and heat until it boils. Simmer, covered, for six hours on low heat. **(2)** After straining, pour the broth back into the pot. To taste, add salt and fish sauce. Maintain warmth on low heat. **(3)** Simply follow the steps on the package to make the rice noodles. **(4)** Place noodles in dishes and add raw steak sirloin on top. To cook the meat, ladle hot broth over it. **(5)** As garnish, serve with bean sprouts, lime wedges, sliced chiles, and fresh herbs on the side.

PHO WITH RED WINE VINEGAR REDUCTION

Preparation Time: 15 minutes || Cooking Time: 30 minutes || Servings: 4

Ingredients:

8 cups beef or chicken broth	2-star anise
1 cinnamon stick	1/4 cup red wine vinegar
3 tablespoons sugar	1 tablespoon soy sauce
200g rice noodles	1/2 lb cooked chicken or beef, shredded
Fresh herbs, bean sprouts, lime wedges, and sliced chili for garnish	

Instructions:

(1) Add sugar and red wine vinegar to a pot. On medium heat, thicken and reduce by half. Set aside. **(2)** Bring the broth, cinnamon stick, and star anise to a boil in a big saucepan. Stir in the red wine vinegar reduction and soy sauce. Allow to simmer for twenty minutes. **(3)** Simply follow the steps on the package to make the rice noodles. **(4)** To serve, transfer the shredded meat and noodles into dishes. Spoon hot stock over. Add some bean sprouts, Chile, lime wedges, and fresh herbs as garnish.

WORCESTERSHIRE SAUCE CHICKEN PHO

Preparation Time: 15 minutes || Cooking Time: 1 hour || Servings: 4

Ingredients:

8 cups chicken broth	1/4 cup Worcestershire sauce
1-star anise	1 cinnamon stick
2 cloves garlic, minced	200g rice noodles
1/2 lb chicken breast, thinly sliced	Fresh herbs, bean sprouts, lime wedges, and sliced chili for garnish

Instructions:

(1) Enter star anise, cinnamon stick, garlic, Worcestershire sauce, and chicken stock into a large pot. Drop heat and simmer for 45 minutes after boiling. **(2)** Cook the chicken slices for a further fifteen minutes or until they are well done. **(3)** Simply follow the steps on the package to make the rice noodles. **(4)** To serve, put noodles in dishes, then top with chicken and liquid. Add some bean sprouts, Chile, lime wedges, and fresh herbs as garnish.

SAMBAL OELEK

Preparation Time: 10 minutes || Cooking Time: 5 minutes || Servings: Makes about 1 cup

Ingredients:

1 pound fresh red chili peppers, roughly chopped	2 teaspoons salt
4 cloves garlic, peeled	1 tablespoon distilled white vinegar
1 tablespoon sugar (optional)	

Instructions:

(1) Put the garlic, chili peppers, and salt in a food processor. Pulse the machine a few times to make small pieces. **(2)** Move the blend into a pot, include the vinegar, and sugar if desired. Cook for approximately five minutes, or until the mixture slightly thickens, over medium heat. **(3)** Once the sambal oiled has cooled, move it to a jar that has been sterilized. You may keep it in the fridge for up to one month.

GOCHUJANG

Preparation Time: 30 minutes (plus fermentation time) || Cooking Time: 2 hours || Servings: Makes about 2 cups

Ingredients:

1 cup dried chili flakes	2 cups water
1 cup sweet rice flour	1 cup soybean powder (mau-mau)
1 cup malt barley powder	1 cup sugar
½ cup sea salt	

Instructions:

(1) Combine the chili flakes with one cup of water in a big dish and put it aside. **(2)** Stirring constantly, boil sweet rice flour and one cup of water in a saucepan over low heat until a thick paste forms. Let it chill. **(3)** Mix the soybean powder, malt barley powder, sugar, and sea salt with the cooled rice paste. Stir well. **(4)** Mix well after adding the Chile mixture to the paste. **(5)** Fill a glass or clay container with the ingredients. Ferment it under cheesecloth for one to three months in a warm, shady place. **(6)** The completed gochujang can be stored for up to a year in the refrigerator, where it will continue to ferment gently.

KIMCHI

Preparation Time: 30 minutes (plus salting and fermenting time) || Cooking Time: 0 minutes || Servings: Makes about 2 quarts

Ingredients:

1 large Napa cabbage, cut into 2-inch pieces	¼ cup sea salt
Water	4 cloves garlic, minced
1 teaspoon ginger, grated	1 tablespoon sugar
2 tablespoons fish sauce (optional)	¼ cup chili flakes (Korean gochutgaru)
1 daikon radish, julienned	4 green onions, chopped

Instructions:

(1) Transfer the cabbage to a large basin, toss in the salt, and then cover with water. Allow it to soften for around two hours. **(2)** After thoroughly draining, rinse the cabbage under cold water. **(3)** Make a paste with the garlic, ginger, sugar, fish sauce, and chili flakes in a separate bowl. **(4)** To the mixture, add the daikon radish and green onions. After that, add the drained cabbage and stir well to coat every piece. **(5)** Squeeze the mixture tightly to eliminate any air spaces from the jar once it has been sterilized. Make sure the top has a minimum of 1 inch of room. **(6)** For fermentation, cover the jar and leave it at room temperature for one to five days. Once it reaches your desired flavor, put it in the fridge.

FURIKAKE

Preparation Time: 10 minutes || Cooking Time: 5 minutes || Servings: Makes about 1 cup

Ingredients:

½ cup sesame seeds	¼ cup finely chopped nori (seaweed)
2 tablespoons bonito flakes (optional)	1 teaspoon salt
1 teaspoon sugar	2 teaspoons soy sauce

Instructions:

(1) Toast sesame seeds until fragrant and slightly brown in a dry pan over medium heat. Allow to cool. **(2)** Toasted sesame seeds, nori, bonito flakes (if used), sugar, and salt should all be combined in a small bowl. **(3)** Once the mixture is somewhat wet, add the soy sauce and stir thoroughly. **(4)** Place the mixture on a baking sheet and let it dry for approximately one hour. **(5)** Furikake should be kept in an airtight container. It works well as a spice for salads, grains, and soups.

THE END

Printed in the USA
CPSIA information can be obtained
at www.ICGtesting.com
CBHW082213211124
17843CB00028B/514

9 798320 701943